THE BEST OF The MAILBOX® Magazine

Writing

Grades 1–3

Great writing activities and reproducibles
from the 1992 to 2002 issues of
The Mailbox® magazine!

- Revising Ideas
- Seasonal Writing
- Publishing Activities
- Report Writing

- Journal Writing
- Handwriting Activities
- Letter Writing
- Learning Center Ideas

And much, much more!

Editorial Team: Becky S. Andrews, Kimberley Bruck, Karen P. Shelton, Diane Badden, Thad H. McLaurin, Debra Liverman, Sharon Murphy, Karen A. Brudnak, Sarah Hamblet, Hope Rodgers, Dorothy C. McKinney

Production Team: Lisa K. Pitts, Theresa Lewis Goode (COVER ARTIST), Pam Crane, Rebecca Saunders, Jennifer Tipton Cappoen, Chris Curry, Sarah Foreman, Theresa Lewis Goode, Ivy L. Koonce, Clint Moore, Greg D. Rieves, Barry Slate, Donna K. Teal, Tazmen Carlisle, Amy Kirtley-Hill, Kristy Parton, Debbie Shoffner, Cathy Edwards Simrell, Lynette Dickerson, Mark Rainey

www.themailbox.com

D1517593

Manufactured in the United States
10 9 8 7 6 5 4 3 2 1

Table of Contents

All About
Harrisburg
Academy
by Ms. Kulp's
Class

Rachel

T is for toadlet. It means a toad that isn't an adult.

O is for old skin. A toad sheds its old skin.

A is for amphibian. That is what a toad is.

D is for dark because toads can see in the dark.

The dog ran.

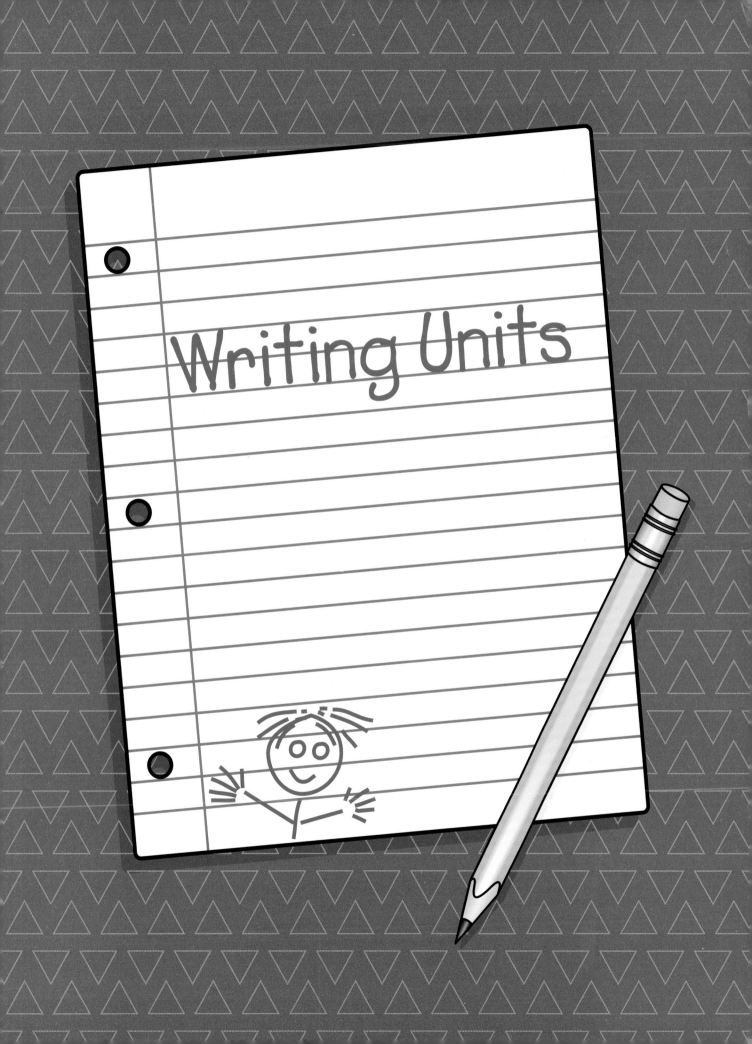

Getting Started on the "Write" Foot!

Step "write" up to the new school year with this collection of easy-to-implement writing activities! Your students' writing skills will be back in business in no time—and there's no fancy footwork involved!

ideas by Lisa Kelly

The "Write" Foot

Get your students started on the "write" foot with these colorful student-made journals. Use the foot pattern on page 8 to make a class supply of journal covers. Place the journal covers, 9" x 12" sheets of construction paper, a supply of 4" x 8" writing paper, scissors, pencils, and a stapler at a center. To make her journal, a student personalizes and cuts out a journal cover. Next, she positions the cutout atop a sheet of construction paper, traces around the shape, and cuts on the resulting outline. Then she staples a supply of writing paper between her two journal covers. Continually keep this center stocked with journal-making supplies so that students can create additional journals as needed. If desired, set aside time each day for students to write in their journals.

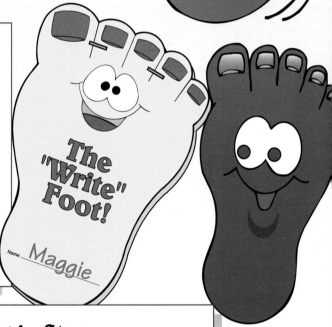

The "Write" Foot!

Name Maggie

Staying in Step

Use a simple animated foot character like the one shown above to keep your youngsters in step with writing all year long!

- For a year-round display, laminate and display the foot cutout and the title "Staying in Step With Writing" on a bulletin board. Have each student display a favorite piece of published writing on the board. Each month, ask students to replace their displayed writing with more current samples.

- For a daily journal-writing prompt, tape the character to the board and draw a large speech bubble beside it. Each day, program the speech bubble with a title, a story starter, or another writing prompt. Students may choose to use the provided writing prompt for journal writing, or they may write about a self-selected topic.

Colorful Counting

Not only does this ten-day journal activity review number words and color words, but it also strengthens question-and-answer skills! Under your students' direction, write the number words from one to ten on a length of bulletin board paper. In a similar manner, create a list of color words. Post the resulting lists for student reference. Give each child a construction paper journal that holds ten sheets of story paper. Have each student write her name and the title "Colorful Counting" on the front cover of her journal and then add other desired cover artwork.

To begin the journal activity, write "How many _____ are there?" on the board. Exhibit one item and ask a student volunteer to orally complete the question. Then ask another volunteer to answer the question, stipulating that the answer must include a number word and a color word. Write the student's answer on the board. Repeat this procedure several times, using a different item each time. Then ask each student to write, answer, and illustrate the modeled question in her journal. Over the next nine school days, spotlight the numbers two through ten in sequential order. In a few days, the students will be eager to identify their own number sets, allowing you to omit this step in the procedure. Later in the year, repeat the activity—this time relating it to the current theme of study. "How many sloths are there in the rain forest?"

How many apples are there?

There are three red apples.

Happy

I was happy on my birthday!

Exploring Emotions

Sometimes youngsters have difficulty identifying the emotions they're feeling. This journal activity invites students to explore and better understand their feelings.

Each child needs a construction paper journal that contains five or more blank pages. Ask each student to title the front cover of his journal "My Feelings" and then personalize it with his name and other desired decorations. To complete a journal entry, introduce an emotion like happy, sad, calm, surprised, or angry. Write the emotion on the board and demonstrate facial expressions and body language that portray the emotion. Encourage students to talk about times they've experienced this feeling. Next, have each child write the emotion at the top of a blank journal page and illustrate a time when he felt this way. Students may also write (or dictate for you to write) about their experiences. Explore a different emotion every few days. When the journals are completed, ask students to continue to store them in their desks. The completed journals can be handy tools for the students (and yourself) when interpersonal conflicts arise.

Handfuls of Achievements!

This weekly writing activity creates a handy year-round display! Each week, ask every student to trace the outline of his hand on colored paper and cut out the resulting shape. Inside the hand cutout, have the child write his name and one accomplishment from the past school week. After each child has shared his accomplishment with the class, display the students' handiwork on a bulletin board titled "Give Us a Hand!" At the end of each month or grading period, ask your students to join you in applauding the entire class for its outstanding accomplishments. Then remove the hand cutouts from the display and send them home with the students so that the accomplishments can be shared with family members.

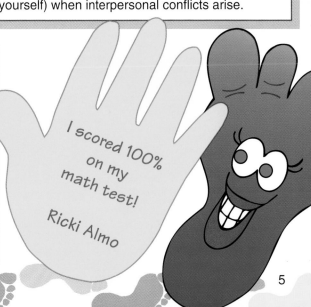

I scored 100% on my math test!

Ricki Almo

A Family Affair

Students will find writing about their family members an enjoyable task. And because this writing activity results in a one-of-a-kind project, the task is even more desirable! Each student needs a white construction paper copy of the paper doll pattern on page 9 for each family member, including himself. On each pattern—in the provided box—a student names and describes a different family member. Then the student cuts out and decorates his patterns to resemble his family members. Provide an assortment of arts-and-crafts supplies for decorating that includes crayons, yarn, buttons, scraps of fabric, construction paper, and wallpaper. Remind students to not decorate over their writing. To assemble his family booklet, a student arranges his decorated cutouts side by side in a desired order. Then, working from left to right, he glues each tab to the adjoining cutout. The student trims off the final tab and his project is complete. Have the students form a sharing circle so that each youngster may introduce his family of cutouts to his classmates. If you're preparing for open house, be sure to display these one-of-a-kind family projects for your visitors to enjoy!

What a Walk!

I Went Walking, written by Sue Williams and illustrated by Julie Vivas, is a perfect springboard for a beginning-of-the-year writing activity. This easy-to-read picture book chronicles the colorful critters that a small boy encounters while on an innocent stroll.

For an independent writing activity, have each student copy the sentences "I went walking" and "What did I see?" near the top of a 9" x 12" sheet of drawing paper. Instruct each child to illustrate her paper by drawing herself and part of the animal she plans to see. Suggest that the students picture themselves (and the partially hidden animals) in the animals' natural surroundings. Next, have each student copy, complete, and illustrate the sentence "I saw a [color] [animal] looking at me" on the back of her paper. Assemble the students' work into a class book titled "We Went Walking." No doubt your students will take a walk to the classroom library to check out this class publication!

If you prefer to follow up your oral reading of *I Went Walking* with a group activity, try this! For each group, you will need a length of white paper labeled with the sentences "We went walking" and "What did we see?" As a class, brainstorm places where the students would like to walk, such as a beach, a city, a forest, and a jungle. List the students' ideas on the board. Next, divide the class into groups. After each group has chosen a different place to take its walk, distribute the lengths of paper that you've programmed. Ask the members of each group to use crayons or markers to illustrate their length of paper to show the things they imagine seeing on their walk. Display the resulting artwork for all to see. Older students can write the name of each illustrated item on a blank index card and then tape the cards to their group's artwork near the corresponding illustrations.

A hospital in Edina, MN, is where I was born on May 17, 1997.

Beautiful is the word my parents used to describe me.

Alphabet Autobiographies

Teach your students the ABCs of writing autobiographies with this unique approach. At home, have each student research special events from her life; then have her bring her findings to school. On separate sheets of paper, ask each child to write autobiographical sentences that begin with different alphabet letters. Challenge older students to create a sentence for each letter of the alphabet. Then have each child illustrate her pages and design a book cover for her book. To complete her book, a student sequences the pages alphabetically and then staples them between her book covers. Right down to the letter, these autobiographies are a great way for students to record their special memories.

Candy Whelan—Gr. 3, Garlough Elementary
West St. Paul, MN

A Happy Class!

Reinforce happy thoughts with a class happy book. To make this class journal, cut out and staple a supply of circular writing paper between two construction paper circles. Draw a happy face on the front cover. Program the first page with the title "Our Happy Book" and the current date; then place the journal and a special pen (perhaps one with happy faces on it) at a writing center or other desired location. Near the end of each school day, select a different student to write several sentences in the journal that describe a happy event from his day. Ask each child to sign and date his journal entry. Periodically write happy entries in the journal yourself. Then set aside time every week to read aloud the entries for everyone to enjoy. You'll find that these happy thoughts have a very positive effect on the ambience of your classroom! When the journal becomes filled with happy thoughts, make another one. If desired, make the completed journal available for overnight checkout.

Shirley Smith—Gr. 3, Lincoln Elementary, Huntington, IN

Pam Crane

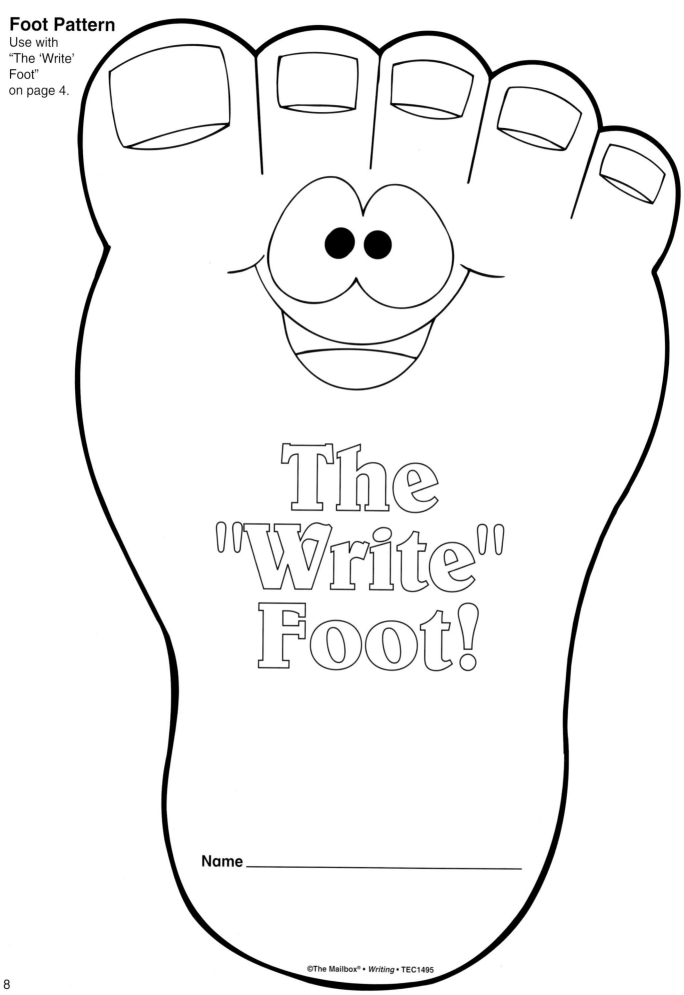

Foot Pattern
Use with
"The 'Write'
Foot"
on page 4.

The "Write" Foot!

Name _____

Building a Classroom of Writers

Create a blueprint for writing success with these easy-to-use ideas!

Lay the Foundation

Choose from the suggestions on pages 10–12 to establish a class writing routine complete with helpful tools for your young authors!

Lights, Camera, Writing!

Give the writing process a starring role! Title a separate poster-size sheet of paper for each stage of the writing process used in your classroom. Add brief explanations of the stages and then embellish the posters with star cutouts. Display the posters side by side in consecutive order. Then outline the posters with a film-like border, and add "Take" labels and a titled director's board as shown. Explain to students that moviemaking involves many takes, with a director making decisions and changes at each stage in the process. Point out that many authors use a similar process when they write. Direct students' attention to the display and review the steps it outlines. Encourage youngsters to use the display as a writing guide. Student writing that earns rave reviews is sure to be the result!

Pam Sanderson—Gr. 2
Davis Drive Elementary
Apex, NC

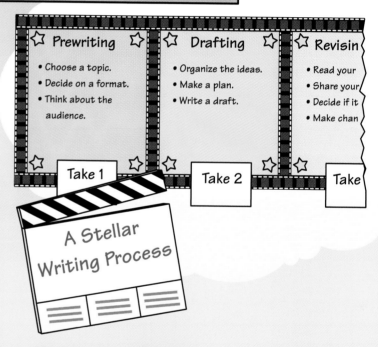

Prewriting
- Choose a topic.
- Decide on a format.
- Think about the audience.

Take 1

Drafting
- Organize the ideas.
- Make a plan.
- Write a draft.

Take 2

Revisin
- Read your
- Share your
- Decide if it
- Make chan

Take

A Stellar Writing Process

"Soup-er" Writing

Set the stage for first-rate writing with this literature-based idea! Read aloud Marc Brown's *Arthur Writes a Story*. In this installment of the Arthur Adventure series, the beloved aardvark gains a new perspective about what makes a great story. At the conclusion of the book, prompt discussion about why Arthur's pet story is better received than his more outlandish tale. Next, display a jumbo kettle-shaped cutout labeled "'Soup-er' Writing." Have students brainstorm qualities of excellent writing, such as vivid details or a beginning that hooks readers. Record their ideas on the cutout. To encourage further exploration of these qualities, place an empty recipe box and a supply of blank recipe cards near the poster. When a youngster reads a book that exemplifies one of the listed qualities, have her describe on a card how the quality was shown, write the book title, and then deposit the card in the recipe box. On a designated day each week, share any newly deposited cards with students. Then post the cards around the cutout. Not only will students become better writers, but they'll also become more thoughtful readers!

Sonia Armstrong—Gr. 2, Thomas J. Lahey Elementary, Greenlawn, NY

At a Glance

It's a snap to manage a writers' workshop with these two colorful displays!

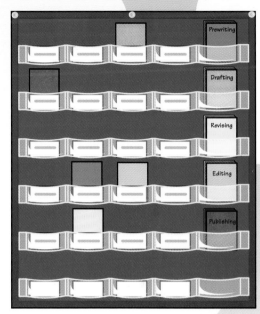

Pocket Chart: Write each student's name on a separate 1" x 3" card. Arrange the cards behind the clear plastic pockets of a store-bought pocket chart so that every name is visible. Designate a different color for each stage of the writing process and then cut a class supply of 3" x 3" cards for each color. Store the cards as shown, placing a labeled card in the front of each stack to make a color key. Instruct each student to tuck a blank card of the appropriate color behind his name to indicate where he is in the writing process.

Kathleen Gillin—Gr. 2, Cold Spring Elementary, Doylestown, PA

Clothespin Lineup: For each stage of the writing process, label a colorful 4¹/₂" x 12" poster board rectangle and laminate it for durability. Also prepare a poster board rectangle labeled "I'm Stuck!" to use when students want teacher guidance. Attach the top of each rectangle to the edge of a shelf or another accessible location that allows for clothespins to be clipped along the bottom of the rectangles. Have each youngster clip a personalized clothespin on the rectangle that reflects his current stage in the writing process.

Jennifer Boone—Gr. 3
Bethel Elementary School
Bethel, PA

Seasonal Signals

This seasonal display doubles as a management tool! Use yarn lengths to divide a bulletin board into three columns; title them as shown. Label a separate seasonal cutout for each student. Use pushpins to tack the cutouts in the first column. During a class writing session, if a student is making headway with her work and does not need teacher guidance, she leaves her cutout in the first column. If she wants to meet for teacher feedback or arrange to share her work with the class, she moves her cutout to the appropriate column. (Be sure the student understands that she should continue writing—either on the current piece or a new one—while she waits for a turn.) After a youngster meets or shares, she returns her cutout to the first column. A quick look at the board reveals who needs teacher assistance!

Katherine Phelan—Grs. 1–2
Frances Xavier Warde School, Chicago, IL

Authors' Briefcases

It's easy for students to get down to the business of writing with these convenient carriers! To make an author's briefcase, attach loops of masking tape to the front of one pocket folder. Align a second pocket folder atop the taped folder and firmly press the two folders together. Open the resulting briefcase. Use clear tape to secure the outer edge of the joined folders as shown. Also tape tagboard handles inside the front and back covers of the briefcase. Then label the pockets to correspond with the class writing process. Have each youngster personalize his briefcase and then use it to store his work in progress. No more misplaced papers!

Cindy Schumacher—Gr. 1, Prairie Elementary, Cottonwood, ID

Joe's Writing Briefcase

Writer's Toolbox

How can your young authors maximize their writing time? By keeping the tools of the trade close at hand! Explain that every writer needs the right supplies to do his job. But because no two writers are exactly alike, the supplies they need vary. Write a student-generated list of possible writers' supplies on the board. Possibilities include sharpened pencils, lists of hard-to-spell words, and souvenirs that provide inspiration. Next, have each student create a toolbox in which to store his writing supplies. To do so, ask him to bring in a lidded shoebox (or a box similar in size). Provide a variety of arts-and-crafts materials and have the youngster use them to decorate his box. Then guide him in stocking it with helpful supplies. Have the student store the toolbox in a designated classroom area for easy access.

Karin Thompson, Easton, PA

Seeds for Stories

Students' writing is sure to blossom when they have a supply of personally chosen topics! Provide each student with a 4½" x 12" construction paper strip and several quarter sheets of blank paper. Direct the youngster to fold the strip in half. With the fold at the top, have her insert the stacked paper and then staple along the fold. Ask her to title the resulting notepad "[Name]'s Seeds for Stories." Encourage each student to keep a watchful eye for story topics wherever she goes. Have her jot down observations, questions, ideas—any notes that have the potential to grow into stories. When it's time to start a new piece of writing, she will have plenty of intriguing ideas to choose from!

adapted from an idea by Lona Burnett—Gr. 3
Ocean Breeze Elementary
Indian Harbour Beach, FL

new boy in our class

bird nest outside my window

Aunt Jane's surprise visit

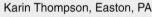

Begin Construction

Help students shape their writing with the top-notch ideas on pages 13–14!

Writing With Purpose

Here's an idea that provides a powerful purpose for writing—an audience! Before your youngsters begin writing, ask each student to think of a person whom she would like to read her work. Suggest a parent, an older sibling, or an adult neighbor. Have each youngster complete her writing, using the established classroom routine to revise and edit it. Then provide her with a copy of a form similar to the one shown. The student completes the top portion of the form and staples it to her writing. She shares her work with the chosen reader at a mutually convenient time. The youngster returns her work and the completed form by a predetermined date. Then she stores the materials in a writing folder for a motivational reminder of an appreciative reader!

Pamela Cobler Packard, Campbell Court Elementary, Bassett, VA

September 20

Dear *Mr. Bartlett,*
Here is a story that I wrote. It is called "The Perfect Weekend." I would love for you to read it! Please let me know what you think.

Sincerely,
Mindy

Reader: *Mr. Bartlett*
Relationship to the author: *neighbor*

The thing I like most about the story is the surprise ending. I didn't expect it at all!

Decisions, Decisions!

Poems, letters, stories of every sort—writing can take countless forms! To investigate the possibilities, display a variety of written materials, such as fiction books, pamphlets, and newspaper articles. Share them with students, explaining that each one represents a different writing format. Further explain that every author should use a writing format that is suitable for his readers and the information he wants to share. Next, post a sheet of chart paper titled "Writing Menu." Have students brainstorm writing formats; record their suggestions on the chart. Throughout the year, encourage your youngsters to consult the resulting writing reference for ideas (and inspiration!).

Paragraphs Beyond Compare

Comparing and contrasting is as easy as 1, 2, 3 with this paragraph plan! Draw a large Venn diagram on the board and label it with chosen topics. Enlist students' help to write information in each section of the diagram. Next, model on an overhead projector how to use the diagram to write three paragraphs. To do so, use the details that are unique to each topic in two separate paragraphs. Then use the details they have in common in a third paragraph. Provide time for students to practice using the same framework with self-selected topics. As they become more proficient, guide them to include opening and closing paragraphs in their work.

Josephine Flammer, Bay Shore, NY

A Story That Hits the Spot

This reproducible idea helps students cook up stories organized to perfection! Draw on the board a hamburger with lettuce. Lead students to identify the parts that hold it together (the top and bottom buns), the main part (the hamburger), and the special ingredient (the lettuce). Then challenge students to explain how a hamburger is like a story. After students share their ideas, give each youngster a copy of page 15. Use the sheet to clarify students' understanding of the analogy. Then have each youngster use the reproducible to plan a story about a topic of her choice. Provide time for her to later complete the story on provided paper. Now that's an idea made-to-order for young writers!

adapted from an idea by Goldy Hirsch—Special Education, Grs. 1–3
Beacon School, Brooklyn, NY

Story Strips

Put a comical spin on prewriting! To prepare, program a full sheet of paper with six blank comic strip frames. Copy the sheet to make a class supply plus a few extra. Clip selected comic strips from the newspaper. Read each strip aloud for students' listening enjoyment. Then ask students to verbally compare comic strips with fiction books. Lead them to conclude that both genres can be used to tell a story with a beginning, a middle, and an end. Comic strips show stories scene by scene, however, and do not provide much detail. Reread a previously shared comic strip, pausing after each frame for students to suggest details that could be incorporated if a longer version of the story were told. Next, give each youngster a copy of the prepared comic strip frames. Have him use the frames to block out an original story with sketches and notes, leaving any unneeded frames blank (provide additional copies as necessary). When it's time to further develop the story, the student will have a handy guide from start to finish!

Tara Kenyon
Medford, MA

Name _____

A Story That Hits the Spot

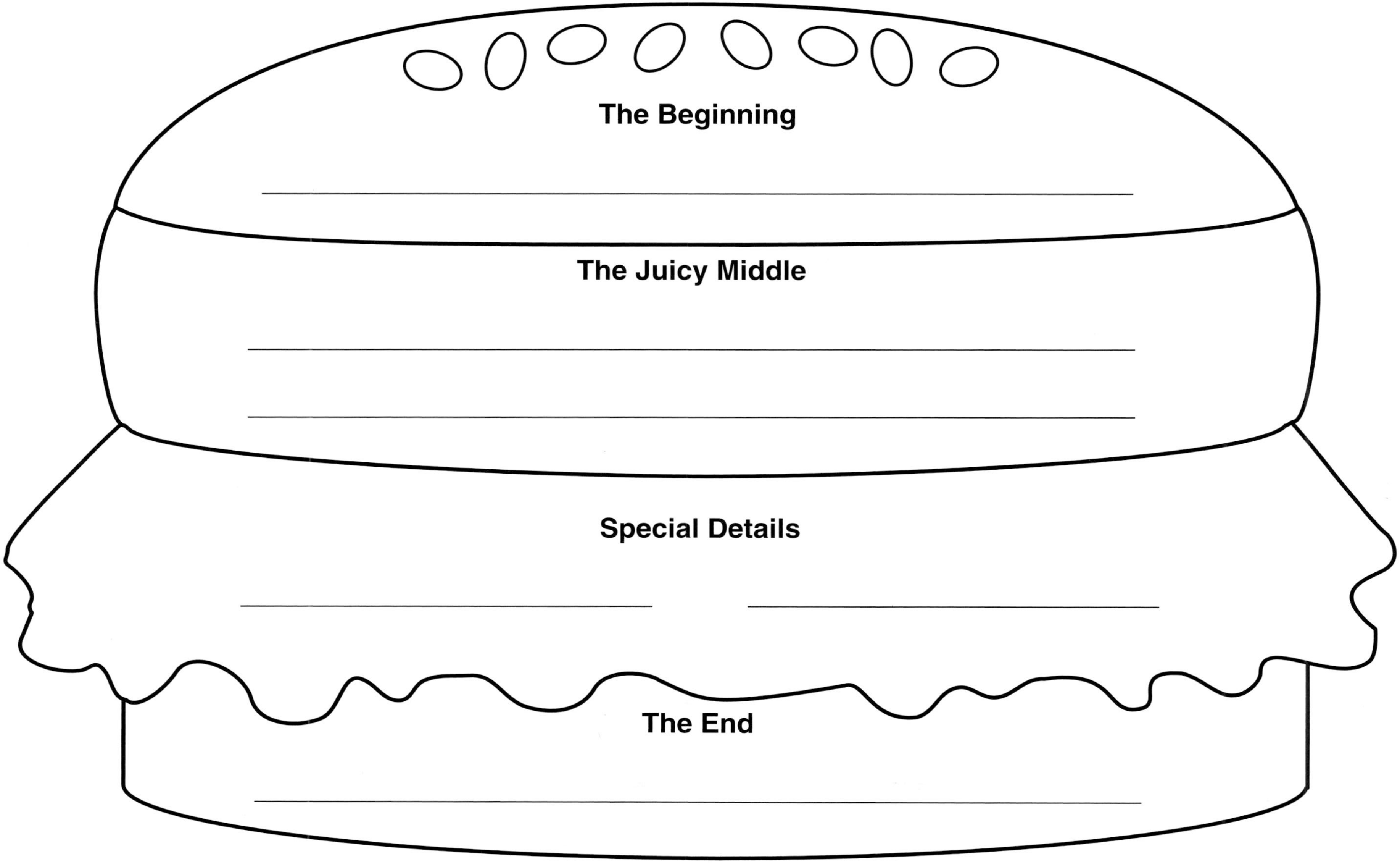

The Beginning

The Juicy Middle

Special Details

The End

Note to the teacher: Use with "A Story That Hits the Spot" on page 14.

15

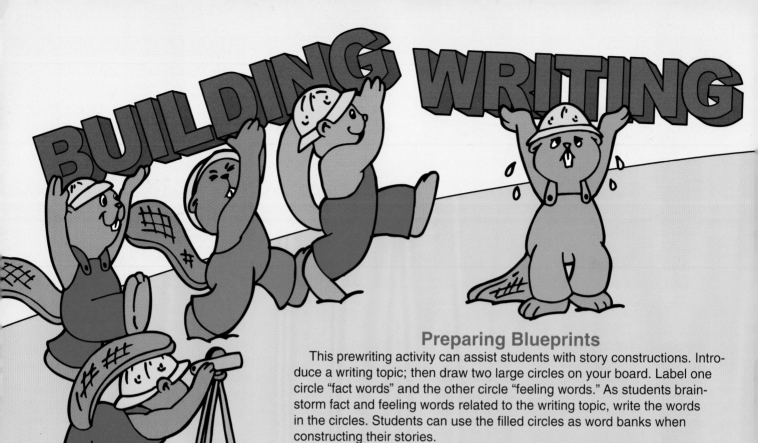

BUILDING WRITING

Preparing Blueprints

This prewriting activity can assist students with story constructions. Introduce a writing topic; then draw two large circles on your board. Label one circle "fact words" and the other circle "feeling words." As students brainstorm fact and feeling words related to the writing topic, write the words in the circles. Students can use the filled circles as word banks when constructing their stories.

Extend this activity by drawing and labeling four circles with the following: "people, places, or things" (nouns); "action words" (verbs); "describing words" (adjectives); "when and where words" (adverbs). Proceed with the activity as described above.

The Writer's Toolbox

This story structure activity will have your crew writing stories in a snap! Write each sentence of a three-sentence story on a separate sheet of paper. Label the backs of the sheets "beginning," "middle," or "ending" to correspond with the story sequence. Place the sheets inside a toolbox.

Present your writer's toolbox to students, explaining that the toolbox contains three necessary tools for story construction. Unveil the tools separately, examining the fronts and backs of the sheets. With student assistance, turn these "tools" into a story.

Assist students as they construct stories of their own. Have students fold large sheets of story paper into thirds, as shown, and then cut on the folds to create three sheets of story paper. Label the backs of the sheets to match those in the toolbox; then provide time for students to construct their stories. Finished stories can be stapled together.

A Writer's Checklist

Experienced writers can benefit from a writing checklist like the one on page 18. Provide students with copies of the checklist, instructing them to check off each guideline as they evaluate their writing. This writing step would precede the proofing step and eliminate careless mistakes. The checklist may be expanded to fit the needs of your writers.

Beginning Builders

Young writers can find writing success with rebus stories. Begin building around simple words such as *a, the, is,* and *has.* Encourage writers to draw rebus pictures or use inventive spellings for unknown words. This writing process removes the anxiety that is often associated with writing. The stories may then be illustrated and shared if desired. Challenge older writers to use rebus pictures to replace the nouns or verbs in their stories.

SKILLS

It's time to roll up your sleeves and begin building writing skills! You'll find easy-to-follow blueprints for a successful writing program along with reproducibles and an award on the following pages. You've won the bid on this building contract!

by Mary Anne Haffner and Sue Ireland

The Final Touches

Proofreading, or adding the final touches, is a step that can be taken at any grade level. Provide each student with a copy of the proofreading card on page 18. With student assistance, display and proof three-sentence stories. Provide further proofing practice by duplicating three-sentence stories for students to proof independently and then check together. Provide colored pencils or fine-tip markers for students to use when they begin proofing their own stories.

Students can also work as editing partners. After a student has edited his partner's work, he writes a note to his partner that includes a positive sentence about the story and one writing suggestion (if applicable). The partners may then work together to correct spelling and punctuation errors.

Writing Exhibits

Showcasing your writers' completed work in a variety of ways will bring rave reviews! These suggestions require a minimal amount of preparation:

- Place stories (complete with title pages) in clear, plastic report covers. Display the stories in your room or school library.
- Copy stories of young writers onto chart paper (using colorful markers); then mount the stories on poster board and laminate them. Display the stories independently or create a big book of stories by binding the laminated stories together with metal rings.
- Schedule times for writers to share stories with students in other classrooms.
- Ask your librarian to host Meet the Authors Day. A videotape presentation can feature interviews of student writers (informing others about why they enjoy writing, how they think of ideas, or writing tips) and a sampling of their works.

Tools of the Trade

Give student writers access to a variety of writing tools by setting up a permanent writers' corner in your classroom. Gather a thesaurus, a dictionary, alphabet stamps, a proofreading chart, a writer's checklist, an old typewriter, and a variety of writing paper to place in this special area. And, of course, you'll need a toolbox for storing items such as markers, crayons, pencils, erasers, and stickers! Encourage writers to visit this area at their leisure. If possible, designate an area near your writers' corner for displaying student stories year-round. Along with providing a special writing area, you'll be providing terrific writing motivation!

Name _____

My Writing Checklist

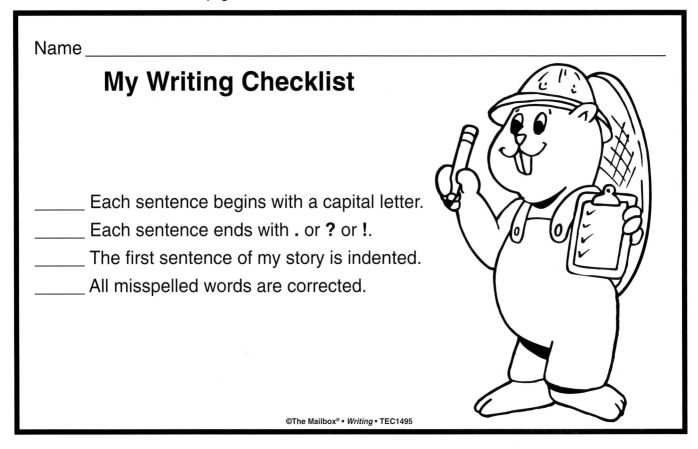

_____ Each sentence begins with a capital letter.

_____ Each sentence ends with **.** or **?** or **!**.

_____ The first sentence of my story is indented.

_____ All misspelled words are corrected.

©The Mailbox® • *Writing* • TEC1495

Award
Use after completing the activities on pages 16–17.

Congratulations!

_____
Student

on becoming a
Master Craftsperson
of process writing!

_____
Job Site Foreperson

_____
Date

©The Mailbox® • *Writing* • TEC1495

Proofreading Card
Use with "The Final Touches" on page 17.

The Final Touches

Proofreading marks:

≡ = **A capital letter is needed.**

╱ = **A lowercase letter is needed.**

⌿ = **Take this out.**

∧ = **Add this.**

◯ = **Check the spelling.**

be ◯soore◯ ∧to proof
your ~~be~~
Writing
carefully.

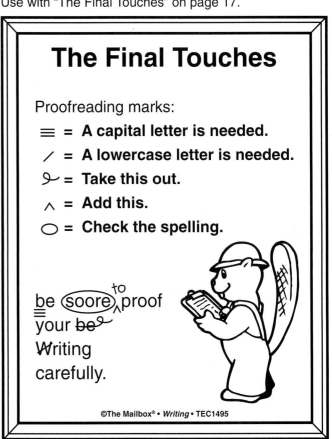

©The Mailbox® • *Writing* • TEC1495

18

Writing Tune-Up
Helping Students Revise Their Writing

Fuel your young authors' independence and steer them toward success with this collection of revision ideas and tips!

Tools of the Trade

Choose from the suggestions on pages 19 and 20 to outfit your students with handy writing tools, and shift the revision process into high gear!

Shop Talk

How do professional authors get their writing all spiffed up and ready to go? Author Eileen Christelow knows. She shares many of the answers in *What Do Authors Do?* Read the book aloud; then point out that the main characters use several different strategies to revise their writing. Display a sheet of chart paper that you have titled as shown. Ask students to recall the characters' strategies for improving their writing. List the responses on the poster. Invite students to make additional suggestions based on their own writing experiences, and add these ideas to the list. Then display the completed poster to provide a helpful reference of top-notch revision strategies.

What Authors Do When They Revise

- Cross out words.
- Read to other people and get feedback.
- Change words.
- Use carets to add details.
- Listen, watch, and think.
- Research to get more information.
- Change the order of things.

Drafts

Golden Revisions

Golden Motivation

Add a golden touch to the writing process, and motivate even your most reluctant writers to revise their drafts! Label each half of a white shirt box, as shown, to make two paper trays. Stock the drafts tray with white paper. Embellish the second tray with adhesive gold stars and stock it with yellow paper. Place the trays in an established classroom writing area. Have students use the white paper for first drafts and the yellow paper for revised drafts. If desired, prepare a third paper tray labeled "Fancy Finals" and stock it with decorative paper for publishing students' writing. Now that's a paper trail bound to inspire high-quality writing!

Linda Masternak Justice
Kansas City, MO

Awesome Author's Folder

There's no doubt about it—revising goes more smoothly when an author has all of her work neatly organized! To help your students organize their writing in progress, give each student two manila file folders that have different one-third cut tabs. The youngster places one folder inside the other and staples the folders together close to the outer fold. Next, she labels the tabs, as shown, and personalizes the front of the resulting multisection folder. Then she tapes a provided writing checklist or rubric inside the front cover. The student can easily refer to her brainstorming or a previous draft as she revises her writing. Plus, she can see the pride-boosting progression of her work!

adapted from an idea by Toni Rivard—Gr. 3, Somerset Elementary
Somerset, WI

Color-Coded Paragraphs

Brighten the revision process with highlighters! In advance, select two short paragraphs from a grade-appropriate science or social studies textbook. Copy them on a sheet of chart paper, trading one sentence in the first paragraph with one sentence in the second paragraph. If desired, insert an irrelevant sentence or two. To begin, remind students that every sentence in a paragraph should be about the same main idea. Also explain that paragraph organization is one thing that writers double-check.

To demonstrate an easy way to check paragraph organization, display the prepared writing and read it with the class. Then have students identify the main idea of the first paragraph. With students' help, use a highlighter to mark every supporting sentence. Use a different-colored marker to repeat the process with the second paragraph. Point out that the color coding reveals at a glance which sentences belong together and which, if any, sentences should be omitted in a final draft. Encourage students to use this colorful organization strategy with reports and other selected writing assignments.

E. Ashley Rebman—Gr. 2, The Christ School, Orlando, FL

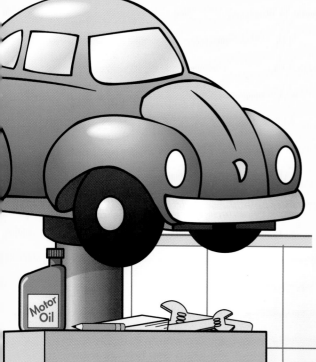

Tune-Up Tip: Writing Models

Look no further than your classroom library for a source of stellar writing models! When a student notices a great story lead or a vivid description, have him mark the corresponding page with a sticky note. Periodically invite volunteers to share their findings with the class. Before long, your young writers will strive to imitate their favorite authors!

Repairs and Polishing

Use the ideas on pages 21 and 22 to help students patch their writing with missing details and enhance it with just the right words!

Colorful Words

Students take their writing to new heights with the help of this ongoing display! Select a word that students often overuse, such as *little, pretty,* or *said.* Write the word on a blank white card and glue it near the top of a colorful poster-size balloon cutout. Challenge students to brainstorm or consult a thesaurus to identify words that have similar meanings but are more precise. Write the words on the balloon and attach a length of curling ribbon. Tack the balloon to a bulletin board titled "Colorful Words." Throughout the year, enlist students' help to add balloons for other words. When a student is looking for a substitute for an overused word, she'll have a bunch of colorful words to choose from!

Shelly Lanier, Lexington, NC

Author Interviews

Vague and confusing writing becomes a thing of the past with this revision strategy! Write the following sentences on the board: "Suzy played with her cat before school. It was fun." Read the sentences aloud; then remark that you wonder about some of the things that the author left out, such as how Suzy played with her cat, what the cat looks like, and what the cat's name is. Invite students to brainstorm questions for the author that could uncover these details and improve the story.

To follow up, pair students. In turn, each student reads to his partner a story that he has written. The partner asks questions to point out places in the story where additions, deletions, or clarifications might be made. The student author jots down the questions on provided paper and later considers them as he makes revisions. Clearer, more interesting writing will be the result!

Linda Masternak Justice
Kansas City, MO

Slinky Story

A favorite children's toy is just the ticket when it comes to helping young writers strengthen their story ideas! Hold a closed Slinky spring toy in your palm. Suggest that when it is closed and compact, it is not very interesting. Then slowly open the Slinky toy and point out that it becomes more intriguing as it is stretched out. Explain that a piece of writing is similar because important details stretch out the writing and make it more entertaining. Caution students that good authors carefully select the best words and details to give readers the full picture rather than add words simply to make stories longer. When holding conferences with your students about their writing, remind youngsters to remember the Slinky toy!

Linda Rudlaff—Gr. 3, Nuner Elementary
South Bend, IN

What happened next?

Word Wonders

What a difference a word makes! Draw a T chart on the board and label the columns as shown. Nearby, write a sentence frame similar to the one shown. Then, in the appropriate columns, write student-generated adjectives and verbs that could be used in the sentence. Have students use various combinations of the listed words to create a number of different sentences, changing the verb tenses and adding words as needed to be grammatically correct. Discuss as a class how the word choices can dramatically change the meaning of the sentence. After this activity, students will look at their own word choices more critically!

Nancy Anderson, Troy, OH

adjectives	verbs
beautiful	dances
young	flies
injured	rests
magnificent	

The _____ butterfly _____ flower.
The magnificent butterfly danced by the flower.
The injured butterfly rests on the flower.

Take Three!

This simple idea helps young writers manage a key part of the revision process: word choice. Ask each student to silently read a draft of a story that she has written. Have her circle three words that she could replace to make the story clearer or more interesting. Next, pair students. In turn, each youngster shares her work with her partner and asks the partner to help brainstorm substitutions for the circled words. The youngster writes the suggestions on provided paper and tucks the notes in her writing folder for later reference. When it's time to make revisions, she'll have a clear-cut focus and plenty of helpful suggestions at her fingertips!

Linda Rudlaff—Gr. 3, Nuner Elementary, South Bend, IN

Get the Picture?

Drawing and writing are a perfect combination when it comes to revising story details! Give each student one sheet of drawing paper. At the bottom of the paper, have the youngster write "The dog ran." Then instruct him to illustrate the sentence. Invite each student to show the class his illustration. Next, ask students to share their observations about the variations among the illustrations. Lead them to conclude that many differences are due to the lack of specific information about the setting, the dog, and the dog's behavior. Revise the sentence with students' input so that it creates a clearer visual image.

To give students additional practice with using words that create clear pictures, ask each youngster to take home a sheet of drawing paper and a draft of a story that he is writing. Have the student read his story to a family member and ask his listener to sketch the visual image it creates. Instruct the youngster to study the illustration to determine which story details need clarification and then revise his work accordingly.

Jan Robbins, Fairview Elementary School, Richmond, IN

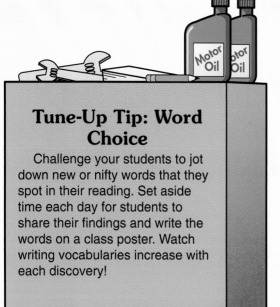

Tune-Up Tip: Word Choice

Challenge your students to jot down new or nifty words that they spot in their reading. Set aside time each day for students to share their findings and write the words on a class poster. Watch writing vocabularies increase with each discovery!

The dog ran.

The dog ran.

Test Drive

Set students on the road to productive peer conferences and self-assessments with these ideas!

Writing Gems

Here's a gem of a writing checklist! Suggest to students that a piece of writing is like a diamond—it's a bit rough or plain at first, but with skillful work and a final polish, it can really shine! Distribute copies of the writing checklist on page 24 and review the questions with the class. Ask each student to store a copy of the checklist with his writing materials. Before he seeks feedback on a piece of writing, encourage him to complete the checklist and make any indicated revisions. Keep copies of the checklist on hand to help youngsters develop plenty of well-polished stories!

Kathleen Scavone, Middletown, CA

Expert Advice

Set the stage for peer conferences with this class activity! In advance, write a poorly developed story on an overhead transparency sheet. Tell students that every writer (even an adult!) benefits from feedback. Explain that the most helpful type of feedback points out strengths as well as areas for improvement. Tell students that you have written a story and would like their input. Display the prepared story and read it aloud.

Next, invite youngsters to tell what they like about the story and why. Then encourage them to suggest improvements, such as adding details or using more specific words. List students' comments and suggestions on a sheet of chart paper. Later, consider students' advice as you revise the story. Share the new and improved version of the story with the class. You can be sure your young critics will be proud to have helped!

adapted from an idea by Elizabeth Searls Almy
Greensboro, NC

Ruler Rubric

How does your older students' writing measure up? Find out with this nifty rubric! Give each student a copy of the rubric on page 24. Discuss the listed criteria. Then, as a class, use the rubric to rate anonymous pieces of writing or selected passages from children's books. After students are familiar with the rubric, instruct each youngster to keep her copy in an accessible location. Have her use the rubric to size up her completed stories and keep track of her writing growth.

adapted from an idea by Elizabeth Searls Almy

Tune-Up Tip: Peer Conferences

Display a guide like the one shown to remind students how to confer with their classmates. Peer conferences will be letter-perfect!

Kathleen Scavone

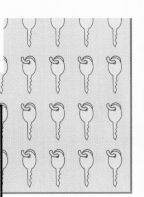

The ABCs of Peer Conferences

A: Ask questions.

B: Be a good listener.

C: Comment thoughtfully.

Rubric

Use with "Ruler Rubric" on page 23.

Checklist

Use with "Writing Gems" on page 23.

Name _____

Writing Gem Checklist

Did I...

- ☐ tell everything in the best order?

- ☐ use interesting details?

- ☐ take out details that are not important?

- ☐ use words that help make a clear picture?

- ☐ write complete sentences?

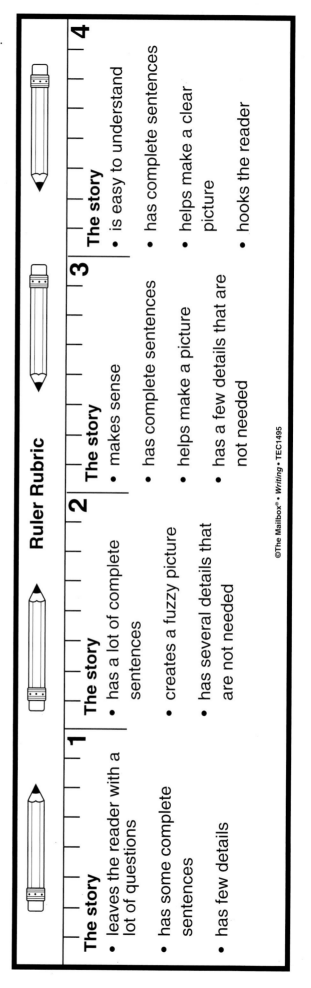

Ruler Rubric

1

The story
- leaves the reader with a lot of questions
- has some complete sentences
- has few details

2

The story
- has a lot of complete sentences
- creates a fuzzy picture
- has several details that are not needed

3

The story
- makes sense
- has complete sentences
- helps make a picture
- has a few details that are not needed

4

The story
- is easy to understand
- has complete sentences
- helps make a clear picture
- hooks the reader

Straight From the Hive

"Bee-Dazzling" Ideas for Classroom Publishing

Do you find yourself wishing you had some fresh ideas for writing motivation, bookmaking projects, and publishing your youngsters' literary accomplishments? Well, thanks to our "bee-loved" subscribers, this honey of a unit is swarming with suggestions!

Monthly Newsletter

Have you ever considered publishing your youngsters' literary efforts in a monthly parent newsletter? In addition to listing students' birthdays, units of study, upcoming events, and suggestions for skill reinforcement, feature several student-authored selections. Students will be thrilled to find their pieces in the newsletter and will be continually motivated to write quality stories, poems, and reports for possible publication.

Nancy Wojcik—Gr. 2
Hayes Elementary School
Kennesaw, GA

Big Book Picture Show

Publishing big books is a major writing accomplishment for youngsters. Rather than simply shelving the books when the writing project is completed, consider republishing the books in the following manner: Photograph the front cover and each page of a child's big book; then have the resulting negatives made into slides. Using a slide projector, a screen, and optional background music, each author narrates a slide presentation of his big book project. Students are certain to enjoy sharing their work through this unique media. Gee, why not take this show on the road?

Andrea Johnson—Grs. 1–2
Rawlings Elementary
Pinellas Park, FL

Classroom Collectables

Sweeten your youngsters' enthusiasm for classroom publishing by displaying their work in an exclusive corner of the classroom. Arrange a bookcase and/or coffee table, a sofa, padded chairs, or pillows in the chosen corner. Display your students' books in the area, taking care to spotlight the most recent publications. Books published by your previous classes could also be made available for perusing.

Leslie Simpson
San Diego, CA

Rave Reviews

Strengthen the home-school connection and boost your youngsters' writing confidence using this one-of-a-kind plan. In a parent letter, explain that each child will be bringing home his most recently published book. Ask that the parents read the books, write positive reviews about the books, and return the books and reviews to school by a designated date. When all of the reviews are in, have each child read the review that was written about his book. Outstanding!

Kim Byrd—Gr. 3
Deer Run Elementary
Dublin, OH

Pam Crane

The Weekly News

Here's a publishing idea that's certain to receive rave reviews. On a sheet of poster board, create a newspaper form like the one shown below. Laminate the form. You will also need a supply of wipe-off markers in a variety of colors. To introduce the project, ask students to recall important or interesting events from the past school week. List these events on the board; then, with your youngsters' input, write the weekly headline and article, and complete the remaining features. Ask one student volunteer to illustrate the weekly headline and another to create a cartoon strip in the spaces provided. Post the completed project outside your classroom door. A week later, wipe away the programming and repeat the activity. If desired, group older students in newspaper staffs and have the staffs create the weekly newspapers on a rotating basis.

Dianne Neumann—Gr. 2
Frank C. Whiteley School
Hoffman Estates, IL

Roepke's Publishing Company

Wow! A genuine publishing company! Each week, ask students to submit a writing sample to your publishing company. Place the youngsters' work in personalized file folders. At the end of six weeks, remove each student's work from his file folder and bind it between construction paper covers. Have students illustrate and personalize the covers of their "published" books. After students have shared their latest literary releases with their families and friends, display them in your classroom library.

Kim Roepke
Tullahomer, TN

Writing to Go

These classroom publications won't be gathering dust! Purchase a supply of three-ring binders. Each time your youngsters complete a writing project, compile their work in a binder. Ask a student volunteer to create and insert a corresponding title page. Using an established checkout system, students may take these published works home to share with their families and friends.

Barb Sandberg—Gr. 2
Christ the King School
Browerville, MN

Student Anthologies

This grown-up approach to publishing keeps youngsters as busy as bees. Discuss what an anthology is with your youngsters; then have each student label a colorful folder "[Student name]'s Anthology." When the folders are decorated, store them in a central location. Throughout the year have students select literary pieces to place in their personalized folders. By the year's end, each student has an outstanding anthology to his credit.

Penny Blazer—Gr. 1
Penns Valley Elementary
Spring Mills, PA

Schoolwide Sharing

Published authors deserve to be recognized! To promote your young writers, make arrangements for them to visit other classrooms to share their written compositions. Or invite neighboring classrooms to your room for informal author readings. Students who prefer to avoid the limelight may choose to loan their books to neighboring classrooms or to the school library for independent reading.

Diane Afferton—Gr. 3
Chapin School
Morrisville, PA

Neumann News
Tadpoles Hatched!
Math Marvels
Really Fun Reading!
Artist Discovered!
Book Review
Comics

By Invitation Only

Add a touch of elegance to book-sharing events by inviting a special guest to each reading celebration. Guests might include your school principal, the police chief, a local author, or a radio or television celebrity in your area. Your students and their guests will feel honored to be a part of these unique celebrations.

Barb Sandberg—Gr. 2

About the Author

Spotlight student authors with easy-to-complete author pages. Make a supply of author pages like the one shown. Also photocopy a supply of each child's school picture. A student glues a copy of his school picture in the box and completes the page using current information. Then he includes the page at the back of his published book. Students feel like real authors and enjoy the recognition they receive as a result of these personalized pages.

Denise N. Morgan—Gr. 2
Kildeer Countryside School
Northbrook, IL

All About the Author

Name __Karl Santos__
Age ____8____
Hobbies __soccer,__
__rock collecting__
Other published books
__The Peanut Butter Alien__
__Undersea Treasure__

Poetry on a Badge

If your school has a badge maker, take advantage of this unique poetry-publishing idea. Following the directions provided with your badge maker, help each student publish an original poem on a badge. These publications will be worn with pride!

Pamela Schmieder—Gr. 2
Wilson Elementary
Zanesville, OH

Our Favorite Pieces

With this method of publishing, students can easily share their favorite literary pieces. All you need is a three-ring binder containing a plastic sleeve for each student. When a student wishes to publish a story or other written work, he simply slips it inside a plastic sleeve in the classroom binder. Later, when he is ready to publish a different selection, he replaces the previously published piece with a more current writing sample. If desired, students may also publish accompanying illustrations. This classroom collection is sure to be well read by students and classroom visitors.

Stacy Barrett Stuttard
Allegheny 1
Altoona, PA

Year-Round Binder

Durable, economical, and versatile accurately describe this year-round publishing strategy. All you need is a large three-ring binder, a supply of top-loading 9" x 12" plastic protectors, and several tabbed divider pages (optional). Decorate the cover of the binder as desired. To publish a literary work, a student obtains a plastic sleeve from you, slips his writing inside, and places it in the binder. If desired, label tabbed dividers with literary categories such as "Poetry," "Mysteries," and "Autobiographies," and ask students to publish their compositions in the appropriate writing categories. When the existing binder becomes full, simply introduce a new one. Keep your distinctive collection of published works on display at all times.

Andrea Lau
Doyle-Ryder Elementary
Flint, MI

Thematic Presentations

Notably conclude your thematic studies with theme-related literary presentations. Invite a neighboring classroom, your youngsters' families and friends, or other desired guests to attend each presentation. If appropriate, encourage students to dress in theme-related attire. You might also consider serving theme-related refreshments. Ask students to share their favorite theme-related writing, such as poems, stories, and reports. Or have students write and perform a theme-related play for their guests. The possibilities are endless!

Leslee McWhirter—Gr. 1
Mendel Elementary
Houston, TX

Night
Night is like a bat flying in the sky.
Night is like the stars falling on me.
I love night,
The night falling on me.
Stacie Welch
2005

Fantasy Stories

To set the stage for writing fantasy stories, ask each student to bring to school the front panel of a cereal box that features a make-believe character. Then have each youngster write and illustrate a story about himself and the fantasy character. Bind each completed story between a cereal box panel (front cover) and poster board back cover of equal size. When the projects are completed, plan a before-school breakfast. After the meal, invite students to share their cereal box adventures.

Donna Tobey—Gr. 1
Gulliver Academy
Coral Gables, FL

Booklets Galore!

Just the sight of dozens of uniquely made blank booklets can provide tons of writing motivation. With the help of volunteers, keep a supply of blank booklets on hand at all times. Books of different sizes and shapes are most appealing. Covers made from colorful construction paper, poster board, and wallpaper and bound with different types of rings and yarn add to the books' charm. When a student is ready to publish a piece of writing, he simply chooses a book and copies and illustrates his edited version of the story inside.

Juliann S. Thrush—Gr. 1
Dream Lake Elementary School
Apopka, FL

Involving Parents

Classroom publishing can create huge demands on a teacher's time. Involving parents in the publication process helps you meet the writing needs of your youngsters. Throughout the school year, recruit and train adult volunteers to assist you with a variety of publishing needs, such as gathering materials, making booklets, and having conferences with individual writers. Parents could even be asked to maintain and run a bookmaking center in your classroom. Everyone benefits when you share the load.

Linda Benedict—Gr. 2, Indian Lake Elementary, Huntsville, OH

Dorothea Uniacke—Gr. 1, Fisher School, Walpole, MA

Schoolwide Publishing Center

Rather than having a "publishing company" in each of several classrooms in your school, why not join forces with your teaching colleagues and open a schoolwide publishing center? In the center, store desired cover-making supplies, including a laminator and a bookbinding machine. Ask parent volunteers to assist you in setting up and maintaining the center. When a student has written and illustrated the pages of his book, he visits the publishing center. Here an adult volunteer assists him in making a cover. If desired, title pages, dedication pages, and author pages could also be completed at the publishing center.

Michele Lasky—Gr. 1
Mandalay Elementary School
Wantagh, NY

Writing Extravaganza

Turn your youngsters on to writing with a bit of glitz and glitter! Equip a writing center with a variety of colorful pens and pencils. Also provide materials for making and decorating unique booklet pages. For example, provide several large patterns and a supply of colorful writing and construction paper. Students can create shape booklets by tracing the patterns onto the paper and then cutting out, decorating, and stapling together the resulting shapes. Crayons, markers, glitter pens, rubber stamps, and stamp pads can be used to decorate the booklet pages.

Michele Lasky—Gr. 1

Wordless Publications

For a creative alternative to the writing process, consider having your youngsters publish wordless books. Begin by "reading" and discussing a wordless picture book like Mercer Mayer's *Frog Goes to Dinner*. Then have each student brainstorm a series of pictures that tell a story. Ask each student to draw a rough sketch of each picture he plans to include in his wordless book. Next, pair students and have them discuss their projects and make any desired revisions. Then have each student work individually to complete the final drawings for his book. Bind the completed illustrations between construction paper covers. Give each youngster the opportunity to share his completed project with his classmates.

Diane Fortunato—Gr. 2
Carteret School
Bloomfield, NJ

Book-Assembling Party

Keeping a publishing center equipped with plenty of ready-to-use booklets is a time-consuming task. While parent volunteers are usually willing to help out in this area, the job can become mundane. For a change of pace, invite the parents to your home on a Saturday afternoon for a bookmaking party. In addition to making loads of books for your publishing center, you'll have a wonderful time becoming better acquainted with your volunteers.

Nancy Dunaway

Publicizing Publications

Follow up your students' next publishing project with a media campaign. After displaying their completed books in the school library, have your young authors design eye-catching posters advertising their latest publications. Make arrangements for students to display their completed posters throughout the school. Your authors' readership is sure to increase!

Nancy Dunaway

Springtime Tea

As the school year comes to a close, take time to applaud the accomplishments of your student authors at an authors' tea. Announce the upcoming event in a parent letter; then make arrangements for parent volunteers to provide appropriate refreshments. During the tea, each student shares her favorite published work from the school year. This event will definitely receive two thumbs-up from the audience and the participants!

Carol C. Greenlund—Gr. 3
Camp Hill, PA

Familiar Faces

Your youngsters' book illustrations can take on a whole new look with this clever idea. Make a supply of your students' most current school photographs. Cut apart the reproductions and store them in personalized envelopes at a center. If a student wishes to feature himself or one of his classmates in an illustration and does not wish to render the facial portion of the picture himself, he simply cuts out and attaches a photocopy of the person's school picture. The illustrations often prove to be quite interesting!

Denise N. Morgan—Gr. 2
Kildeer Countryside School
Northbrook, IL

Author Celebrations

Periodically commemorate the literary accomplishments of your student authors with surprise author celebrations. Serve simple refreshments and ask each youngster to read aloud his latest publication. This bit of recognition goes a long way toward keeping your student authors motivated.

Nancy Dunaway
Hughes Elementary School
Hughes, AR

Hooked on Journals

When we asked our subscribers to share their favorite journal activities, we quickly learned that teachers everywhere are hooked on journals! Whether you're just starting to use journals or you're a seasoned pro, take a look at the following teacher-tested tips and activities.

Special Entries

Sometimes children write journal entries that they especially want their teacher to read, but they are too shy to mention them. To resolve this situation, ask students to fold down the top corners of these journal pages. At a glance you can see which entries are top priority.
Denise Evans—Gr. 2, Hodge Elementary, Denton, TX

Clip Art

Inspire creative journal writing with appealing clip art. Cut out a supply of interesting pictures from old magazines and newspapers. Make student copies of each picture. Periodically distribute a set of pictures for a journal-writing exercise. Have each student glue his picture to a journal page and write a corresponding entry. Encourage students to write a variety of entries, such as stories, poems, songs, letters, and personal anecdotes.

Vareane Gray Heese, Omaha, NE

The Literature Link

Combine journal writing, literature, and cooperative learning with this teaching suggestion. Divide students into cooperative groups and give each group member a writing journal, a list of literature-related writing topics, and a copy of the same trade book. During each group meeting, students reflect on their previous reading assignment and share their latest journal entries. Before the group dismisses, it determines the next day's reading assignment and selects a journal-writing topic. The group can choose a writing topic from the provided topic list or concur on an original one. This teaching strategy enhances students' comprehension and writing skills in a positive setting.

Cindy Ward—Gr. 3, Webster Elementary, Rushville, IL

All-About-Me Keepsakes

These yearlong writing journals become treasured keepsakes at the end of the school year. On the first day of school, present each youngster with a writing journal. On that day and every school day during the year, have students write journal entries that reveal something about themselves. For example, writing topics might include "The Funniest Day of My Life," "The Five Best Things About My Family," and "Something I Really Dislike." Ask students to suggest additional writing topics.

Cindy Ward—Gr. 3

Thematic Writing

Here's a fun way to incorporate journal writing into your thematic units. Decorate a bulletin board with pictures related to your current unit of study. Behind or on the back of each picture, write a theme-related question, thought-provoking phrase, or story starter that can be used as a writing prompt. Each morning, ask your daily helper to randomly choose a picture from the display and read its journal assignment. For added writing motivation, provide youngsters with theme-shaped writing journals.

Andrea Johnson—Grs. K–3
Blanton Elementary
St. Petersburg, FL

Closing Sentences

Journal entries take on a whole new twist with this activity. Rather than providing a story starter or story title, provide the closing sentence for a story. For example, challenge students to write stories that end with sentences such as "That's what friends are for," "They lived happily ever after," and "We all went home for cookies and milk." Students will delight in creating stories to fit the assigned endings.

Nancy Barondeau—Gr. 3
Edmunds Central Elementary
Hosmer, SD

It's My Turn!

Making sure that all youngsters have equal opportunities to share their journal writing is a cinch using this management system. Divide students into four groups. Color-code each group's journals by attaching the same color of adhesive dot to the journal covers. Next, assign each group a journal-sharing day: Monday, Tuesday, Wednesday, or Thursday. Reserve Friday sharing for students who were absent on their designated days.

Donna Gregory—Grs. 1–2
Hodge Elementary
Denton, TX

Journaling Center

This journal-writing center will receive rave reviews from your youngsters. Place your students' journals and a variety of pencils, pens, markers, and crayons at a center. Program the current month of a large wall calendar with daily writing topics; then display the calendar at the center. Students visit the center daily to write in their journals. Students may or may not use the writing suggestion for the day. They also have the option of working alone or with a friend. Write on!

Annette Rupert—Gr. 2
Colorado Christian School
Denver, CO

March 2006						
		1	2	3	4	
5	6	7	8	9	10	11
12	13	14	15	16	17	18
19	20	21	22	23	24	25
26	27	28	29	30	31	

Creative Sharing

Using this plan, you can add variety and surprises to your journal-sharing routine. Label each of several cards with a different sharing option such as "Read to the class," "Read to a friend on your left," "Read to yourself," "Read to a small group," and "Put your journals away." Conclude each of your writing sessions by asking the class helper for the day to randomly choose and read aloud one of the cards. Then have students follow his instructions.

Maureen Pecoraro—Gr. 1   *Sally S. Hangliter—Gr. 2*
Cattaraugus Elementary   *Homer-Center School*
Cattaraugus, NY   *Homer City, PA*

A Traveling Journal

Build a bridge between home and school with a traveling journal—a journal that goes home with a different student each school night. Attach a parent letter to the front cover of the journal explaining that each child's assignment is to write and date an entry on the first available journal page. Be sure to mention that students choose their own writing topics. Also encourage parents to take time to read their children's journal entries and the entries written by other youngsters. This activity generates writing interest and increases parent-child interaction. Parents can plan on the traveling journal visiting their homes approximately once a month.

Donna Gregory—Grs. 1–2

Terrific Topics

Most students love to suggest journal-writing topics, so why not capitalize on this wonderful resource? Place a supply of paper slips and pencils at your writing center and encourage students to submit their ideas for journal-writing topics. Review each submission and place the approved topics in a container on your desk. Each day, ask your class helper to draw a slip from the container and read aloud the day's journal-writing topic. You'll have a wealth of creative ideas and a beaming group of motivated writers.

Stephanie Chamblee—Gr. 3
Lomax Elementary, Deer Park, TX

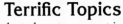

Journal Topics

Sticker Incentives

Your students will be stuck on journal writing with this super incentive program. On the inside cover of each child's journal, attach a 5" x 7" index card labeled "Story Stickers." Each time a child writes a predetermined number of sentences, attach a sticker to her card. When a student's card is filled, she takes it home as a reward for her writing accomplishments.

April Johnson—Gr. 1
Morningside Elementary
Perry, GA

Bunches of Blue Books

College blue books (available in most college bookstores) make wonderful journals for young children. Because college blue books contain fewer pages than most spiral notebooks, students can fill the pages of their journals in less time. This creates an added sense of accomplishment for your youngsters, and it allows parents to review their children's writing more frequently. And to top it all off, these nifty books are inexpensive to purchase!

Joanne Rosengren—Gr. 2
Nashotah, WI

Timely Responses

Reading and responding to students' journal writing is an important factor to consider when implementing a journal-writing program. Here's a system to help you stay on top of this enormous task. Divide your students' journals into four or five groups. Using markers or colorful adhesive dots, color-code each group of journals. Then designate one day per week to read each group of journals. Students will be pleased with your timely responses.

Joanne Rosengren—Gr. 2

The Science Link

Here's a great way to integrate science and writing. In special science journals, have students record their science questions and hypotheses, science experiments, and newly acquired science information. Encourage students to share and discuss their journal entries with one another for increased comprehension.

Kelly McCalla
Oakland Elementary School
Greenwood, SC

Journal Walk

For a fun change of pace, try this unique approach to journal writing. Have each student open his journal to a blank page, write his name at the top, and then lay the journal on his desktop. Then, carrying only their pencils, have students walk silently around the room and write messages, compliments, riddles, and questions in their classmates' journals. When the students return to their desks, they'll have an assortment of messages awaiting them.

Beth Ann Bill—Gr. 3
Lincoln Elementary
Merrill, WI

Welcome to a New Day!

Begin each day with a positive writing experience. Each morning while you are collecting lunch money, student homework, and/or parent notes, have students write in their personal journals. Periodically attach a new list of topics to the inside cover of each journal for extra writing inspiration. As soon as you complete your tasks, begin to write in your personal journal too. Each week, set aside time for journal sharing. In addition, collect students' journals periodically and respond to their ideas and stories by writing brief comments beside selected entries. To reinforce correct spelling, try to include the words that a youngster is repeatedly misspelling in your written comments.

Deb Marciano Boehm—Gr. 2, Woodridge School, Cranston, RI

Fill in the Blanks

Here's a one-of-a-kind journal activity your youngsters are sure to enjoy. Ask each student to write a story on any topic he chooses. The catch to this story-writing activity is that each youngster must replace a predetermined number of key words in his story with blank lines. Then each student takes a turn reading his story aloud. When the student comes to a blank line, he asks a classmate for a word and inserts the word into his story. The resulting tales are truly one-of-a-kind creations!

Beth Ann Bill—Gr. 3

Questioning Journal Topics

For writing motivation, have students brainstorm questions about their writing topics. For example, if the topic is food, students might brainstorm the follwing questions: Who is your favorite lunch partner? What is your favorite breakfast food? Where is your favorite restaurant? When do you like to eat desserts? How often do you eat meals away from home? Students will enjoy generating and responding to these questions.

Julie Minhinnett—Gr. 2
Westview Elementary
Richmond, IN

The Official Journal Prompter

It's official! Choosing writing topics for journal time is the responsibility of the daily journal prompter. You will need an official-looking cap and a decorated box. Place several strips of paper labeled with writing topics inside the box. Each day before journal-writing time, set the container of ideas at the front of the classroom. The official journal prompter for the day then dons the special cap and marches up to the box. He randomly chooses a slip from the container; then, with authority, he proclaims the writing topic for the day. Students will love the presentation and will eagerly await journal-writing time.

Joanne Yantz—Grs. 2–3 Language Resource
Woodfern School
Neshanic, NJ

What's Next?

Keep students actively involved in daily storytime sessions with this journal-writing idea. Each day, conclude the story that you are reading aloud at an extremely exciting or suspenseful part. Then have students predict in their journals what they think will happen next. Encourage students to share their predictions with one another. Everyone will eagerly await the next storytime session.

Julie Vroon—Grs. 1 and 3
Rose Park Elementary
Holland, MI

Writing to the Rescue!

These teacher-tested journal-writing tips and activities are sure to save the day—without a lot of heroic effort!

1, 2, 3!

Increase students' journal-writing motivation with these three suggestions.

- The Buddy System: When writing time is over, have each student pair up with a buddy. Each youngster reads his journal entry to his buddy; then the buddies trade journals and each student writes a positive response in his buddy's journal.
- Open Journals: Have students leave their journals open to their latest entries throughout the day. Journals can be placed on the students' desktops or at a writing center. During the day, students read their classmates' journal entries and jot positive notes to each other in their journals.
- Modeling: Keep a journal of your own and leave it on display for youngsters to read and respond to.

Janiel M. Wagstaff—Gr. 2, Bennion Elementary, Salt Lake City, UT

Topics, Topics, Topics

Add these motivational writing topics to your collection!

- Pretend that you are swimming and you find a treasure chest. Write a story about what is inside the chest.
- Pretend that you are a baseball. Write a story about being in a baseball game.
- Imagine that you and several friends live on a cloud. Write about your life.
- Pretend that you and your family have gone to the ocean. A friendly whale comes along and invites you to ride on its back. Write about your experience.
- Imagine that you have turned into a toy. Write a story about yourself.
- Pretend that you have become an animal for the day. Tell what kind of animal you are and write a story about your day.
- Imagine that you are a newspaper reporter and you discover a footprint that is six feet long. Write a news story about your discovery.

Joanne Yantz—Grs. 2–3 Language Resource, Woodfern School, Neshanic, NJ

A Journal-Writing Corner

Corner your youngsters' creative endeavors at this writing center. Position a desk in a corner of your room. Atop the desk place a timer and a small box. Inside the box place a variety of items such as fabric scraps, small household utensils, and other unusual objects. A child brings her journal and pencil to the center. She sets the timer for five to ten minutes, chooses an object from the box to write about, and writes in her journal until the timer signals that her writing time is over. Change the contents of the box on a regular basis.

Heather Bradley-Mueller—Grs. K–2 Hearing Impaired
Montgomery County IU, Norristown, PA

Field Trip Memories

Enhance the meaning of your class field trips by having students engage in this field trip journal activity. Several days before your field trip, have each student make and decorate an eight-page journal. Then provide the following directions for completing the individual pages. (Pages 1–2 are completed before the field trip. Pages 3–8 are programmed before the trip and completed after the trip.)

Page 1: Write about the upcoming field trip. Include the following information: your name, your teacher's name, your school's name, the location and date of the field trip.

Page 2: Write about what you hope to learn during the trip.

Program pages 3–8 as follows:

Page 3: I saw...

Page 4: Here is a picture of one thing that I saw.

Page 5: I felt...

Page 6: Now I know that...

Page 7: My favorite part of the trip was...

Page 8: I would still like to know...

Encourage students to share their completed journals with their families and friends.

Sandy Bakke, Patton Elementary School, Austin, TX

Mathematical Explanations

Reinforce math concepts with journal writing. After introducing a new math concept, write a corresponding problem on the board. Then have each child write an entry in his journal that explains how to solve this problem. Describing the new math process in writing helps many children solidify their understanding of the concept. This is also an effective way to identify students who are experiencing difficulty in math.

Nancy Barondeau—Gr. 3, Edmunds Central Elementary, Hosmer, SD

Easy-to-Make Journals

These durable journals are easy to make and extremely versatile. To make each journal, staple approximately 20 sheets of story paper between two slightly larger wallpaper covers. (Inquire at your local wallpaper store for a book of discontinued wallpaper samples for this purpose.) Have each student use a permanent marker to personalize his journal cover. Students always have the option of illustrating their written work when these journals are used.

Julie Malin—Gr. 1, St. Albert Primary, Council Bluffs, IA

Vacation Journals

To encourage students to continue their journal writing during school and/or family vacations, send youngsters home with special vacation journals. To make a vacation journal, staple a desired number of blank pages between two construction paper covers. Have each student personalize and decorate the cover of his journal as desired. For best results also send home a parent letter explaining how the journal is to be used. A list of suggested writing topics could also be included. When the students return to school, set aside time for journal sharing.

Mary Ann Cacchillo—Gr. 1, Lafayette School, Shelton, CT

Once Upon a Letter...

Deliver five days of letter-writing fun with this first-class booklet project!

Here's how! Make a class supply of the writing prompts below and cut them out. On each of five days, give each child a copy of one writing prompt, a copy of page 37, and letter-writing paper.

A child writes the letter described in the prompt. To prepare an envelope for her letter, she writes her return address and a make-believe mailing address on her copy of page 37. She also designs and colors a stamp. Next, she cuts on the bold lines and folds on the thin line, keeping her writing to the outside. She glues the outside edges of the folded paper together to create a pocket and then she glues the writing prompt on the back. When the glue is dry, she folds her letter and slips it inside the envelope.

On days 1–4, collect the completed projects. On day 5, after the projects are completed, give each child two 6" x 9" construction paper rectangles. Also return her four previously completed projects. Have each child stack her five projects (addresses facing upward), staple them between the rectangles, and then title and decorate the resulting booklet covers. Getting these first-class booklets home to share with family members is sure to be a top priority among your youngsters!

Leigh Anne Newsom, Chittum Elementary, Chesapeake, VA

Sample Envelope

Writing Prompts

Write a letter to Jack and his mom.
Thank them for the beanstalk plant.
Describe a beanstalk adventure you had.

Write a letter to the three little pigs.
Tell them about a bully who is picking on you.
Ask for their advice on outsmarting the bully.

Write a letter to Cinderella.
Tell her about a new shoe you invented.
Ask her if she would like to order a pair.

Write a letter to the Bear family.
Tell them that Goldilocks visited you.
Explain how things went during her visit.

Write a letter to Rapunzel.
Tell her about a new shampoo you invented.
Tell her why it is perfect for her.

Special Deliveries
From First-Class Pen Pals

Take a fresh look at the learning possibilities that pen pals offer. Whether students correspond across the country or down the hall, or send their messages by postal carriers versus electronically zapping them to their destinations, one thing is clear—the benefits of promoting pen pal correspondence are enormous. So take a few minutes to read our subscribers' suggestions for ways to foster positive pen pal relationships. It's a very special delivery that we feel certain you will enjoy!

Prestigious Pals

If you really want to get children fired up for pen pal writing, try this idea! Survey your class to find out which celebrities interest them the most. Then create a master list of suitable celebrities and their addresses using the following books:

- *The Kid's Address Book* by Michael Levine
- *The Address Book* (10th edition) by Michael Levine
- *2000 Edition V.I.P. Address Book Update* by James M. Wiggins

Duplicate the address list for your students. (If desired, provide additional copies for youngsters to give to their friends.) Then instruct each student to choose a celebrity from the list and write and mail a letter to him or her. Your youngsters will be so thrilled with the responses they receive that they may begin filling up their free time with letter writing!

Iris Blum—Title I Teacher, Legion Park, Houma, LA

Stacey Cashen—Gr. 3 Student Teacher
Ferron Elementary School, Las Vegas, NV

Special Friends

Children who move at midyear can become excellent pen pals. When a student moves away, give him a special note to wish him well and include a stamped, self-addressed envelope. Encourage the student to send you a letter once he is settled. When you hear from the child, ask each student to write a letter to his former classmate. Compile the letters with your letter and send them to the youngster. Students will benefit from the letter-writing experience, and you will have provided a positive model of how to keep in touch with a friend.

Cristy Harts—Gr. 2
Southwest Elementary
Pratt, KS

Who's That Pen Pal?

Foster descriptive-writing skills and stump your students' pen pals with this unique correspondence! Take a picture of each student. When the photos are developed, have each child refer to her snapshot to write a thorough description of herself. Also ask each child to label her letter and the back of her photo with an assigned number. Be sure to create a master list of the number assignments. Collect the photographs and the descriptions; then mail these items along with the master list and a note to the receiving class's teacher. In your note ask that the teacher mount the photos on a bulletin board and distribute the descriptions. Suggest that each child read and reread her pen pal's description until she can guess which photo shows her pal. Using the list you've enclosed, it will be easy for the teacher to verify the matches her students make.

Tina Marsh—Grs. K–5 Gifted
Jefferson Parkway Elementary
Newnan, GA

About Our School

Looking for a unique way to tell your pen pals about your school? Then this idea is for you! Tell your students that you will be working together to make a special booklet to send to their pen pals. First, invite students to brainstorm sentences about their school as you write them on chart paper. Then have each child choose a sentence, copy it onto a sheet of white construction paper, and illustrate it. Collect the completed pages, compile them into a booklet, and drop the project in the mail. Your students' pen pals will proudly display this booklet in their classroom library and perhaps be inspired to reciprocate with a booklet about their school!

Suzanne Kulp—Gr. 2
Harrisburg Academy
Wormleysburg, PA

All About
Harrisburg
Academy
by Ms. Kulp's
Class

News Flash

We interrupt your regularly scheduled pen pal correspondence to bring you the following videotaped news report. "Good morning, pen pals! This is Ryan Lee reporting to you from Silverthorne Elementary School's library. Let's step inside!" For sure, this isn't your typical pen pal correspondence, but you can't beat it for creating interest between pen pals. Have each student select a school location (such as the playground, office, or computer lab) to be the focus of a news report. Encourage each student to write and rehearse an interesting report about the selected area; then videotape each student on location. Set aside time for your class to screen the completed project before mailing it to your pen pals. Hopefully your pen pals will include a news report in their upcoming correspondence too!

Valerie A. Hudson—Title I Grs. 1–5
Silverthorne Elementary School
Breckenridge, CO

Great Connections

This puzzling project gives young letter recipients a lesson in teamwork. Have your students compose a special class message for their pen pals. Then use a marker to write the message on a large piece of poster board. Next, have your students collaborate to create a decorative border around the message. Cut the poster board into pieces and give each student part of the resulting puzzle to include in a letter to his pen pal. Compile the students' letters and a note to the receiving class's teacher in a large envelope for mailing. After the recipients read their letters, they can connect their puzzle pieces to reveal the group message. What a great way to make connections across the miles!

Concetta Maranto—Gr. 3
Sandrini Elementary School
Bakersfield, CA

One of the nation's largest museums of carousel horses is in my town.

Hometown Homework

Give students something to write about by planning this homework assignment. Ask each child to research three facts about her hometown. After sharing her facts with the class, have each child incorporate them into a letter to her pen pal. Your students will think letter writing's a snap when they're armed with interesting things to write about.

Mary Dinneen—Gr. 2
Mountain View School
Bristol, CT

Treasures From Our Town to Yours

Pen pals will be delighted when they receive surprises from your town. Gather a number of artifacts that are native to your town or state (such as information from museums, photos of your town, postcards, and brochures of landmarks). If desired, select a few students to write about the different items. Place the items in a box, along with the letters, and mail them to the pen pals. Your pen pals will treasure their surprises and will likely send some of their town's own artifacts in return.

Suzanne Buza—Gr. 2
Ben Franklin Elementary
San Antonio, TX

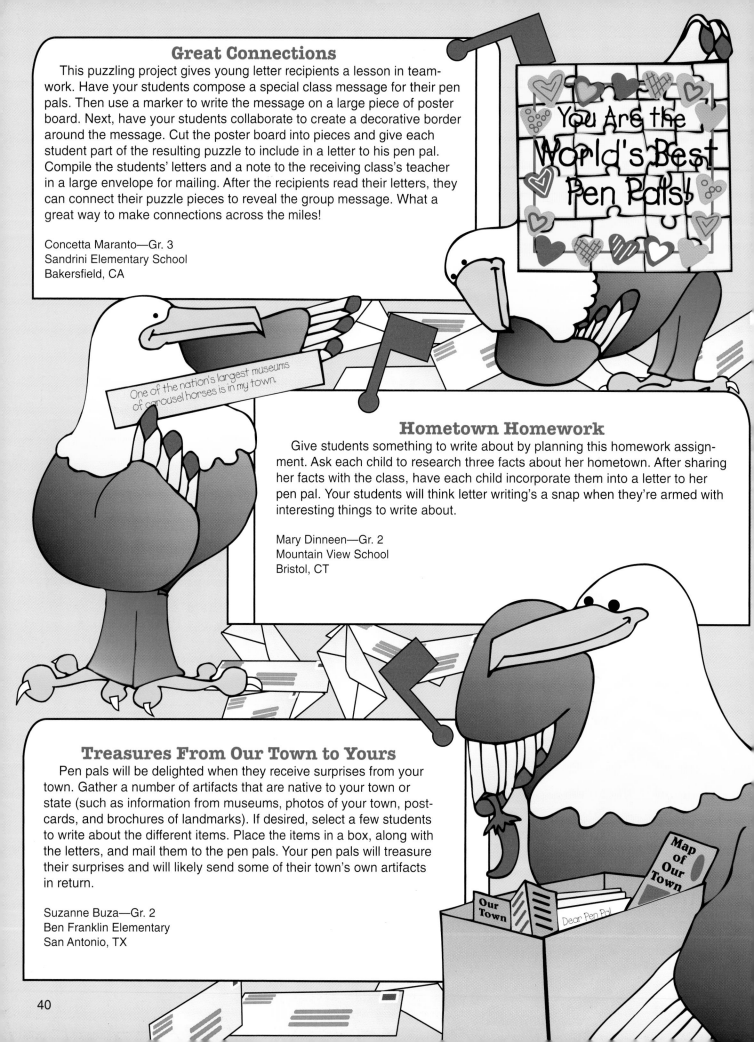

Worth a Thousand Words

When your students write to their pen pals, they'll probably mention classmates—and even you—from time to time. So that the people mentioned in the letters do not remain faceless, use this suggestion. Label a class picture with students' names and your name. Photocopy the labeled photo for each student's pen pal. The next time your students write to their pen pals, have them tuck these photos in the envelopes too.

Carolyn Williams—Gr. 2
North Augusta Elementary
North Augusta, SC

First Row:
Second Row:
Third Row:

Mrs. Williams
Grade Two

Wow!!
He's one
tall dude!

Dear Curtis,
I am 7⅛" tall.
Sincerely,
Sylvester

Celebrity Responses

Engage your students in a graphing activity that has real star appeal. Have each student select a well-known person to write to. (Celebrity addresses can be obtained from the sources listed on page 38.) Ask your class to choose one question for stars to answer, such as "What is your height?" Have each child write the predetermined question on a stamped, self-addressed postcard. (If desired, each student can create his own postcard from boxboard items such as cereal boxes.) Then direct him to enclose it with a letter explaining that the response will be used in a class assignment. When several cards have been returned to students, begin a class graph to chart the responses.

Ritsa Tassopoulos—Gr. 3
Oakdale Elementary
Cincinnati, OH

A Puzzling Idea!

Looking for a playful way to help your students' pen pals put names with faces? Then this idea is for you! Have a photograph of your class enlarged. Glue the enlargement onto poster board. On the back of the poster board, draw lines to create individual puzzle pieces. Then cut the pieces apart. Enclose the puzzle pieces and the original snapshot in an envelope, along with a letter that identifies each pictured person. Mail the project to your pen pals. The receiving class is sure to have a ball as they refer to the snapshot and piece together who their new friends are.

Julie Plowman—Gr. 3
Adair-Casey Elementary
Adair, IA

Just "Write" for the Season!

Pick and choose from this sampler of quick-as-a-wink writing projects!
ideas contributed by Jill Hamilton—Gr. 1, Ephrata, PA

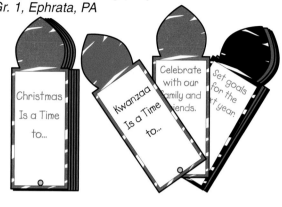

Holiday Highlights

This writing project is aglow with versatility! Each student needs three (or more) copies of page 43. She titles one candle "[Holiday] Is a Time to..."; then—on each of her remaining candles—she completes the sentence in a different way, illustrating her work if desired. Next, she colors and cuts out each candle shape. Lastly, the student stacks her cutouts (placing the titled candle on top) and joins them by poking a brad through each black dot. Happy holidays!

Snowflake Snippets

Most scientists agree that no two snowflakes are exactly the same. So it only makes sense that your students' snowflake snippets—brief student-written tales about snowflakes and the like—will be unique as well! To make a winter writing journal for each child, fold a 9" x 12" sheet of dark blue construction paper in half and staple a supply of writing paper inside. Have each child write "Snowflake Snippets" and her name on the front cover of her journal. On each of several days, provide a different snow-related journal-writing prompt. Follow up each writing session by inviting students to read aloud the snippets they wrote; then have each child cut a snowflake from a three-inch square of white or pastel paper. As students glue their snowflakes to their journal covers, praise the youngsters for the uniqueness of their writings. In just a few days, you'll have created a blizzard of writing interest!

Donna Figurski, Dumont, NJ

Snow-Related Prompts

Pretend you are a snowflake; then...
- write about the neatest place you have landed
- tell how it feels to be part of a blizzard
- describe the advantages of being part of a snowpal or snowball
- explain why you like being different from all the other snowflakes
- write about the loneliest day of your life
- write about the most famous person you have seen

Happy Birthday Biography

Celebrate Martin Luther King Jr.'s birthday with a biography project for beginners. Read aloud a picture book that tells about the boyhood, adult life, and dreams of Martin Luther King Jr. To write a biography about this great man, a student folds a 9" x 12" sheet of blank paper in half three times. Keeping the fold at the top, she designs a cover for her biography. Then she unfolds her paper once and writes and illustrates a fact about Martin's boyhood. She then unfolds her paper again. On each half of the resulting blank paper, she writes and illustrates a fact about Martin's life as a young adult. Then she unfolds her paper one more time and writes about Dr. King's adult life. After the student illustrates her work, she refolds her paper. Her biography project is ready to share!

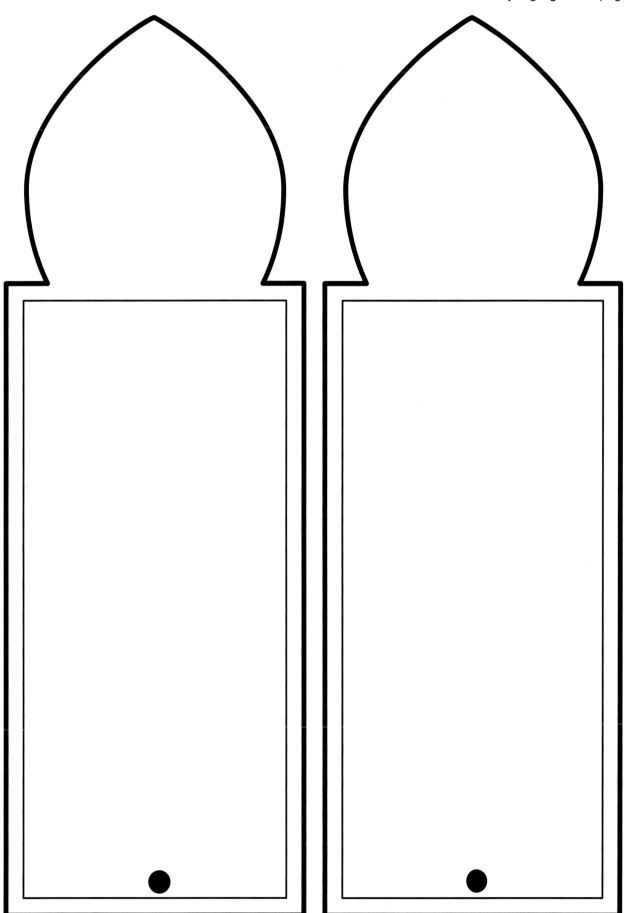

WRITE ABOUT MOM!

Moms are the center of a media blitz when each student creates an original version of a magazine featuring his mother as the Mother of the Year! Have students create the cover and each of the feature pages on different days; then help each youngster staple his pages between his magazine cover. Moms will treasure these special keepsakes for years to come!

adapted from an idea by Ann Wasko—Gr. 3, Windsor School District, Windsor, NY

On the Cover

Moms are definitely cover girl material! To make a magazine cover, have each student draw and color a portrait of his mom on an 8½" x 11" sheet of white paper. Then have him fold a sheet of 12" x 18" construction paper to make a folder and glue his drawing on the cover. Next, have the student attach letter cutouts spelling the magazine's title and add desired cover copy. This issue is sure to be a sellout!

TIME
Exclusive
Karen Price chosen Mother of the Year
Special Edition

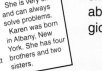

COVER STORY

Karen Price—2005 Mother of the Year!

After a nationwide search, *Time* magazine has chosen Karen Price as the 2005 Mother of the Year.
Mrs. Price is a super mom. She is raising two kids. She is a wonderful cook and is great at cleaning.

She is very smart and can always solve problems. Karen was born in Albany, New York. She has four brothers and two sisters.

Cover Story

Youngsters will enjoy sharing the exciting details of their mothers' lives! To create a cover story, have each student draw, color, and caption a small picture of his mom on his paper. Then have him write a biography about his mom that includes the reasons she was awarded such a prestigious title. Read all about *her*!

INTERVIEW
My Mother Is the Greatest!

Q. What did you think when your mother was named Mother of the Year?
A. I was very happy. My mom is great! I wasn't surprised.
Q. What do you like best about your mom?
A. My mom always helps me. She makes time for me. Also, she is a good cook!
Q. What is the best advice your mom has given you?
A. Mom says to treat others as you would want to be treated.

Exclusive Interviews

Who better to give the inside scoop on moms than their sons and daughters? Make student copies of an interview form similar to the one shown. Have each student illustrate himself and write a caption for his picture. Next, pair students and have them exchange papers. Have each student interview his partner, write his partner's responses, and then return the paper.

SPORTS

Mother on the Move!

Karen Price is a busy woman. She gets her exercise just taking care of her family. Every day she climbs over 300 stairs. She can lift a baby, a dog, and one bag of groceries at the same time!

WORLD RECORDS
• making a bed—30 seconds
• dishwashing—50 dishes in two minutes

Gold Medal Caliber

Even if she never works out at the gym or plays a game of tennis, chances are every youngster's mom hurdles some pretty incredible obstacles getting through an average day. For a sports page, have each student write an article describing some of his mom's inspiring "athletic feats" and then illustrate her engaged in her favorite athletic endeavor. Encourage youngsters to cite special "records" their moms have set. Aerobic grocery shopping, anyone?

The World According to Mom

Youngsters will agree that if moms ran the world, things would be a lot different. Vegetables would always be eaten, and bedrooms would always be clean! For a world page, have each student list several world problems. Below each problem, have the student explain his mom's solution. Then have him complete an illustration of his mom following her own advice. Hats off to moms!

WORLD
Problem-Solving Pro
Tips From the 2005 Mother of the Year

• **Pollution?** Reduce, reuse, and recycle.
• **World peace?** Get rid of guns and bombs.
• **Drugs?** Arrest people who sell drugs.

Recycle Here!

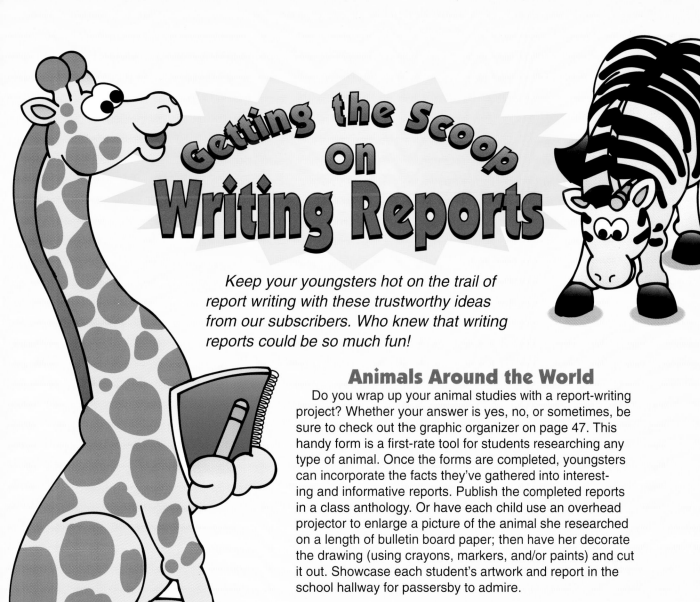

Getting the Scoop on Writing Reports

Keep your youngsters hot on the trail of report writing with these trustworthy ideas from our subscribers. Who knew that writing reports could be so much fun!

Animals Around the World

Do you wrap up your animal studies with a report-writing project? Whether your answer is yes, no, or sometimes, be sure to check out the graphic organizer on page 47. This handy form is a first-rate tool for students researching any type of animal. Once the forms are completed, youngsters can incorporate the facts they've gathered into interesting and informative reports. Publish the completed reports in a class anthology. Or have each child use an overhead projector to enlarge a picture of the animal she researched on a length of bulletin board paper; then have her decorate the drawing (using crayons, markers, and/or paints) and cut it out. Showcase each student's artwork and report in the school hallway for passersby to admire.

Jan Loving—Gr. 2, Forsyth Elementary School, Forsyth, MO

It's in the Name

Just when students think you couldn't possibly come up with a new way to write a report, spring this idea on them! Have each student use a marker or crayon to write the assigned report topic in capital letters down the left-hand side of a sheet of paper. Each child then researches the topic and writes her report by creating a fact sentence for each listed letter. Younger students may wish to follow the pattern "*C* is for…," "*L* is for…," and so on.

Or have each child use a crayon or marker to write the topic at the top of her paper and then write her first name (in capital letters) down the left-hand side. When taking this approach, assign a minimum number of facts that must be included in the report. This means that students with shorter names must include a letter or letters from their middle or last names, and students with longer first names may choose to not write a sentence for each letter in their first names. Your youngsters are sure to have loads of fun using this personalized approach to report writing!

Carol Ann Perks—Grs. K–5 Gifted, Comstock Elementary, Miami, FL

Rachel

T is for toadlet. It means a toad that isn't an adult.

O is for old skin. A toad sheds its old skin.

A is for amphibian. That is what a toad is.

D is for dark because toads can see in the dark.

The Three Rs

Nope! It's not what you think! These three Rs stand for researching, recycling, and reporting. For the research portion, a student chooses an animal to investigate. Then, without mentioning the name of the animal, he writes each of his four favorite facts about it on a separate 5" x 7" card. On a 9" x 12" sheet of construction paper, he illustrates and labels the animal. For the recycling portion, the student uses a recycled paper grocery bag to create a backdrop for his project. To do this, he cuts away the back and the bottom of the bag; then he flattens the bag, keeping the blank side up. He glues one fact card in each corner of the backdrop. He also folds his animal illustration in half and glues it in the center of the backdrop as shown. Then he uses a crayon or marker to write "My Animal Report" and his name on the resulting flap. For the reporting portion, each child, in turn, presents his mystery animal to the class. First, he reads aloud the four facts he wrote. Then he accepts an animal guess from three different classmates. If the animal is identified, he shows the class his illustration. If the animal is not identified, the reporter names the animal and then reveals his illustration. Whether you're wrapping up an animal unit or looking for a unique report-writing opportunity, this project has plenty of kid appeal!

Barbara Cooper—Gr. 1, Tenth Street School, Oakmont, PA

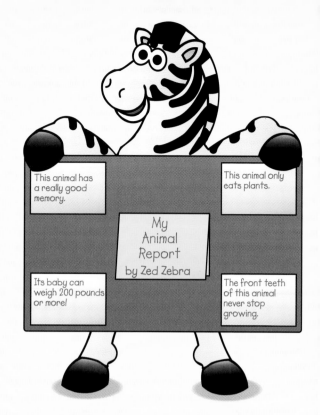

Bugs in 3-D

Students will go buggy over these insect reports! To begin, each child researches an insect and writes each of four fascinating facts about it on a separate 5" x 7" index card. Next, she creates an enlarged three-dimensional replica of the insect. The replica can be crafted in a variety of ways, including forming the bug from salt dough and then painting the dried project, fashioning the bug from modeling clay, or creating the bug from an assortment of arts-and-crafts supplies that might include construction paper scraps, tissue paper, waxed paper, toilet tissue tubes, pipe cleaners, and wiggle eyes. To assemble the report, a student mounts her insect on a cardboard or poster board rectangle that she has labeled with her name and the name of the insect. Then she tapes a fact card to each edge of the rectangle as shown. Display the completed reports around the classroom. Your students will be so proud of their work that you may wish to invite other classes to tour your students' insect gallery. During each tour, have your student reporters stand near their projects so that they can answer any questions that visitors may have.

Rose Zavisca—Gr. 2, South Bend Hebrew Day School, Mishawaka, IN

Working From a Web

When your cub reporters are ready to advance from one-paragraph reports to multiparagraph ones, introduce them to a web. Have each child draw a large oval in the center of a blank sheet of paper and then draw four (or more) straight lines extending from it. Have students write a report topic in the oval; then engage them in brainstorming general ideas about this topic. For example, if the report topic is the ant, general topics might include body, homes, jobs, and interesting facts. List the students' ideas on the board; then have each child copy a different general topic from the list onto each line of his web. As each child completes his research, he notes facts about each general topic on his web as shown. When the note taking is completed, show students how each general topic can be converted into a paragraph by rewriting each general topic as a main idea sentence and each related fact as a supporting detail. Now there's a report-writing strategy that yields interesting reports *and* a better understanding of paragraphs!

Debbie Erickson—Grs. 2–3, Waterloo Elementary, Waterloo, WI

Animal:

Physical Characteristics:

(Give details about what the animal looks like.)

Carnivore   Herbivore   Omnivore

(Circle one.)

(Draw and color a picture of your animal.)

Habitat:

Continent:

Food Chain:

Facts reported by _____

Note to teacher: Use with "Animals Around the World" on page 45.

Now Presenting...
Perfectly Proper Penmanship

Set the stage for handsome handwriting with this spiffy collection of ideas!

ideas contributed by Laura Mihalenko

First Things First

What's the first step in using proper letter formation? Why, using proper posture, of course! Display the provided poem on a decorative chart. When it is time for a hand-writing assignment, lead students in a choral reading of the poem. Encourage them to self-check for each of the criteria before they get to work. When proper handwriting posture becomes more routine for students, prompt them to read the poem silently before they begin a writing task. Ready, set, write!

Get Ready to Write!
Feet on the floor,
Chair pulled in.
Sit up straight.
Now let's begin!

Penmanship Pal

This dapper little mascot provides beginning writers with a helpful reminder about spacing! Use a jumbo craft stick, two wiggle eyes, cray-ons, and glue to make a penguin character like the one shown. Display the completed penguin and introduce it to students as a penmanship pal. Explain that this mascot can help students spruce up their writing with eye-pleasing spac-ing. Demonstrate how to use the width of the mascot to determine the appropriate spacing between the words in a sentence. Then guide each student to make his own penmanship mascot with provided materials. Suggest that he store the completed mascot in a pencil box or another designated area for easy access. After the youngster becomes more proficient at spacing words, have him use the mascot as a visual reminder (rather than a physical guide) by stationing it beside his writing paper.

adapted from an idea by Cindy Schumacher—Gr. 1
Prairie Elementary
Cottonwood, ID

Hats Off to Handwriting!

Give letter-perfect assessment center stage! Post a class-created handwriting scale such as the one shown. Choose a letter to reinforce. Verbally describe its proper formation as you write the letter on a lined chalkboard. Invite students to share their observations about the letter's proper size, slant, and shape. Then give each student a sheet of writing paper. Ask her to brainstorm and write three nouns (or adjectives or verbs) that begin with the featured letter, keeping the criteria for its formation in mind. Have the youngster use the displayed scale to rate each word and draw the corresponding number of hats beside it.

Next, invite each student to read her list aloud. Write the words on the board, avoiding duplications. Chorally read the resulting class list with students; then have each youngster use her best penmanship to copy three additional nouns. For a kid-pleasing conclusion, ask students to rate *your* handwriting. No doubt students will be eager to give this activity a repeat performance, so plan to use it to reinforce other letters as well!

Handwriting Scale

Perfectly proper
Not too shabby
Needs polishing

The Stylish Five

Count on stellar handwriting performances with this ongoing idea! Have each student personalize a folder. At the end of each grading period, distribute copies of the writing paper on page 50. Write the provided prompts on the board, inserting the appropriate month and season. Remind students that neat handwriting has five elements: good spacing, slant, size, shape, and smoothness. Each youngster uses his best penmanship to respond to a selected prompt. After he signs and dates his paper, he colors the illustrations. Then, on a copy of a self-assessment form similar to the one shown, the youngster colors the star for each element that he thinks is well demonstrated in his writing. He elaborates on his assessment in the provided space, staples the form to his writing, and tucks the papers inside his personalized folder. What a "star-ific" way to track students' handwriting progress!

adapted from an idea by Carolyn S. Kanoy
Winston-Salem, NC

Prompts
[Month] makes me think about…
[Month] is a great month because…
My favorite thing about [season] is…
This [season] I…

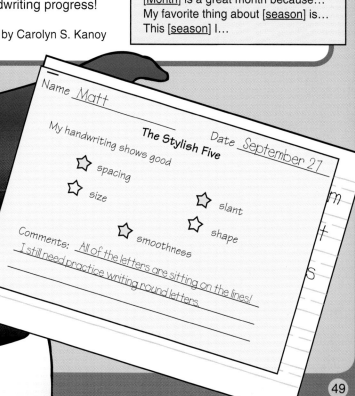

Name Matt

The Stylish Five

Date September 27

My handwriting shows good

☆ spacing

☆ size

☆ slant

☆ smoothness

☆ shape

Comments: _All of the letters are sitting on the lines!_
I still need practice writing round letters.

Name _____

Date _____

Writing Through the Year

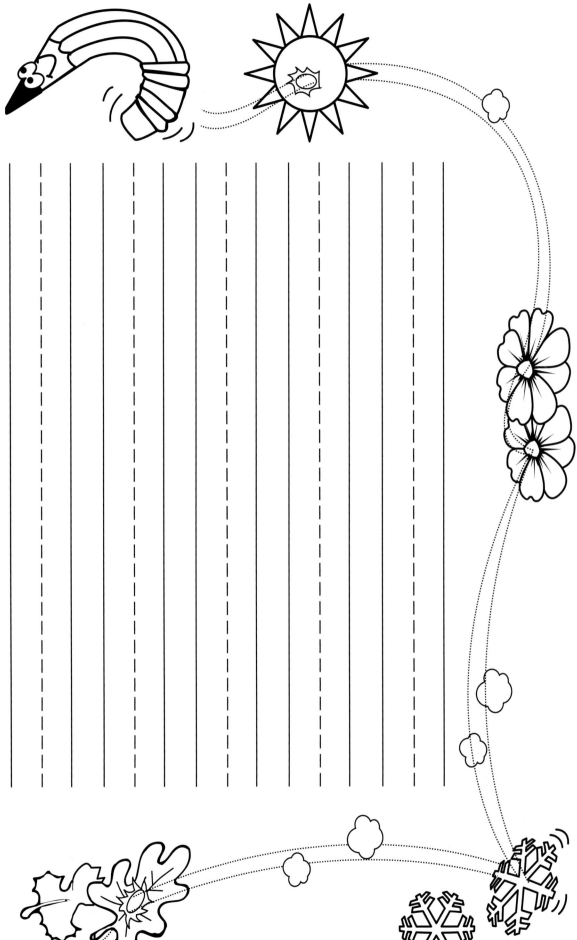

50

Note to the teacher: Use with "The Stylish Five" on page 49.

This sunflower is special because it has purple seeds and it grows to 25 feet! It has purple juice in its stem that makes people smile. It will grow anywhere!

To grow, poke one purple seed in the ground. Water the seed every day until it sprouts. Water the plant two times a day.

Giant Purple-Seeded

Sunflower

Extraordinary Seeds

Students may be surprised that there are more than 60 species of sunflowers! Challenge the class to brainstorm how these species could differ from each other (height, color and size of bloom, leaf shape, growth cycle, and so on). List all ideas on the board. Next, give each child a white construction paper copy of page 58 and ask her to design a seed packet for a new sunflower species. To do this, she illustrates the flower in the oval and writes its name in the boxes. Then, on the provided lines, she writes why the flower is special and how it should be grown. To make the seed packet, she cuts along the bold lines, folds on the thin lines, and glues the tabs as shown. When the glue dries, she drops a sunflower seed inside the packet before she tucks in the top flap. Creativity is sure to blossom!

September 21, 2005

To my grandchildren,
Today I am eight years old. I ride a big yellow bus to school. I use a pencil to a computer too.
shoes cost

Letters for the Future

Here's a first-class letter-writing idea that's sure to please! Ask each child to write a letter to his future grandchildren. Before students begin writing, review as a class several of the changes that have occurred since their grandparents and grandfriends were children. Suggest that students include in their letters the kinds of things they think their future grandchildren will enjoy knowing about them. Then give each student an envelope in which to store his letter. Encourage students to keep their letters safely stored until they themselves become grandparents!

Good Luck Bugs

It isn't clear why ladybugs are thought to bring good luck; however, for centuries people have believed that they do. For an entertaining writing assignment, have each child write and illustrate a tale about a ladybug encounter that results in good luck! Set aside time for students to share their stories; then bind the stories into a class book titled "The Good Luck Bugs."

Apple Autobiographies

Students will have a bushel of fun completing this writing activity! In advance, label each of several apple cutouts (one for every two students) with a different get-acquainted question. Cut each apple shape into four or five pieces and store each puzzle in a sandwich bag. To begin, pair students and give each twosome a puzzle. Students also need pencils and writing paper. Each pair assembles its apple puzzle and reads the question together. Then each child answers the question on her paper in the form of a complete sentence. On a signal from you, the pair rebags its puzzle and passes it to the next twosome along an established route. Continue in this manner until all questions have been answered by all pairs. Ask each student to read her resulting autobiography to the class. You'll learn about your new crop of youngsters, and they'll learn about each other!

Jennifer Neimann—Gr. 2
Hempstead Accelerated School, St. Louis, MO

Just 30 Pounds...

Did you know that during a growth spurt a large pumpkin can gain 30 pounds in a single day? Share this interesting fact with your youngsters. Ask students how their lives might change if they gained 30 pounds of muscle in one day. Then have each student write and illustrate a story about the day that it really happened! Bind the stories into a class-room book titled "It Was Only 30 Pounds!"

Missy

The day I gained 30 pounds of muscle, I scared my mom. I moved the refrigerator! I leaped over our house, and I even carved a pumpkin with my bare hands

Three Parts

How are a story and a piece of candy corn alike? Each one has three parts! Remind your young authors that a good story has a beginning, a middle, and an ending. The beginning of a story introduces the reader to the story's subject, the middle tells something about the subject, and the ending wraps up the tale. Provide a few creative-writing prompts, such as the student who ate too much candy, the disappearing teacher, and the amazing candy corn. Ask each child to select a writing prompt and then, on a copy of the story organizer from page 59, outline how his story will begin, develop, and end. When a child's plan is complete, he writes and illustrates his story on provided paper. Be sure to set aside time for students to share their original tales with the class!

A Beginning
Tell about Jackson. He eats only candy corn.

A Middle
Jackson turns into candy corn! All

An Ending

Turkey to the Rescue!

Wild turkeys have many talents. They can fly fast—up to 50 miles per hour. They can fly high—clearing the tops of 80-foot trees. They can run fast—up to 25 miles per hour. Wild turkeys also have exceptional eyesight and hearing. And, in the right conditions, a turkey's gobble can be heard from up to one mile away! For a fun creative-writing activity, have students incorporate the many talents of a wild turkey into tall tales titled "Wild Turkey to the Rescue!" Ask each child to illustrate his turkey tale before he shares it with the class. Whoa! That's some turkey!

Christmas Candles

In today's Christmas ceremonies, candles are found almost everywhere! Lighted candles adorn churches and homes, electric candles illuminate frosty windows, and colorful candle illustrations embellish greeting cards and holiday gift wrap. Prompt students to pen their thoughts about candles with this writing activity. Give each child a 5" x 8" sheet of writing paper on which to copy the title "A Candle." Challenge him to fill his entire paper with candle-related thoughts. Then have each child mount his completed work on a colorful 6" x 9" sheet of construction paper and glue a bright yellow flame to the top of his project. Showcase the lit candles on a bulletin board titled "Glowing Thoughts."

A Candle

A candle is a pretty Christmas decoration. Most candles smell good. I like to watch the wax melt. A candle is lit by fire, so you must be very careful around it. My dog doesn't like candles very much. I like candles a lot.

The gingerbread man came jogging into Pizza Palace. He started hopping from pizza to pizza. He grabbed a big piece of pepperoni off a lady's pizza. She swung her bag at him! The gingerbread man raced out the door and down the street.

by Joni and Sam

Local Gingerbread Celebrity

You'll be greeted with plenty of enthusiasm when you suggest that students write a story about a gingerbread cutout on the run in the local community! Set the scene by reading aloud a favorite version of *The Gingerbread Man.* After a brief discussion of the story, write a student-generated list of community locations that a gingerbread cutout might visit. Inform students where the story will begin (perhaps in a bakery) and how it will end (the cutout finds safety in their classroom). Then pair the students. Ask one pair to write and illustrate the beginning of the story and another pair to write and illustrate the story ending. Ask each remaining pair to select a different community location from the list and then write and illustrate a story scene that begins with the character arriving at the location and ends with it leaving. Compile the students' work into a one-of-a-kind class book!

Warm Up to Winter!

Showcase warm thoughts with this marvelous mitten display! To begin, have youngsters brainstorm ways to keep warm in cold weather, and record their responses on the board. Then give each student two white construction paper mittens. A child cuts out his mittens and places them on his desk so that the thumbs point to each other. On one mitten, he writes and completes the sentence "To warm up on a snowy day…" He illustrates his sentence on the other mitten. Next, the youngster glues each mitten onto colored construction paper. He cuts around each shape, leaving a narrow border. Then he tapes one end of a length of yarn at the bottom of each mitten and glues bits of cotton to each cuff. Display the mittens with the title "Warm Up to Winter!" Now that's a handy way to pair writing and illustrating!

To warm up on a snowy day, I drink hot chocolate with marshmallows.

A Well-Known Woodchuck

Who's the world's most renowned groundhog? Pennsylvania's Punxsutawney Phil, of course! Each year Phil's spring forecast is a worldwide media event. This year stage your own pre–Groundhog Day event! Collect one clean and empty soda can per student and provide a variety of arts-and-crafts supplies. Challenge each child to transform his can into a one-of-a-kind groundhog. Promote creativity by suggesting that students dress the woodchucks in shadow protection attire (if they're hoping for an early spring).

On the day of the event, have each student take his creation outdoors to an open area and determine whether the groundhog sees its shadow. Then have the students return to the classroom with their groundhogs and generate front-page news! To do this, each child writes "The Groundhog Gazette" and "February 2" and the date on a strip of blank paper. He glues this paper near the top of a full page of newspaper. Next, he pens a newsworthy article about the event on writing paper and illustrates the event on blank paper. He glues these papers to the newspaper project. When the glue is dry, he folds the project in half and presents the paper and his groundhog to his family on Groundhog Day!

The Groundhog Gazette
February 2, 2006

Groovy Greta
Avoids
Her Shadow

reported by Chester Reed

When Greta Groundhog exited her winter den, she wore a red cloak and king-size sunglasses. She carried a shiny umbrella. The crowd cheered. One child exclaimed, "I think Greta read Little Red Riding Hood this winter!" Whatever Greta did worked well. Even though the sun shone brightly, Greta did not see her shadow. Spring is on its way!

A Legendary Holiday

Get to the heart of Valentine's Day with a class book project! Invite students to share their ideas about the origin of this holiday, explaining that no one knows for sure how it began. Next, ask each student to write and illustrate a legend that tells how he thinks Valentine's Day started. If desired, have him mount his legend on a sheet of paper that he has sponge-painted with holiday colors. After each youngster reads his legend aloud, share the age-old legends that are provided. Then bind the students' projects into a class book titled "Getting to the Heart of Valentine's Day."

Age-Old Legends About the Origin of Valentine's Day
- Long ago, the Roman emperor did not allow marriages. A priest named Valentine defied the emperor and married young couples. After Valentine died, the holiday was named for him.
- When a man named Valentine was jailed in ancient Rome because of his religious beliefs, his friends sent him notes. Valentine's Day was later established in his honor.
- Once there was a holiday for Juno, queen of the Roman gods and ruler over marriage. This day was celebrated as a holiday of love.

Special Shamrocks

Saint Patrick is honored because, despite many hardships in his life, he was loving to everyone. Give each student the opportunity to follow Saint Patrick's lead and show someone that he cares. Lead students in a discussion of the reasons that they care for others. Next, give a copy of the shamrock pattern on page 60 to each child.

To make a shamrock, have each child choose an adult whom he cares about and compose a letter explaining the reasons. Then each student colors his shamrock, cuts it out, and glues it on green construction paper, trimming as desired. Invite students to take their completed shamrocks home and present them to their honorees. What a special way for a child to show that he cares!

Bunny Tales

Keep your students' writing skills in tip-top shape with these student-made bunny journals. To make the journal cover, a student folds a 6" x 9" piece of brown or white construction paper in half to 4½" x 6", trims away the bottom corners, and unfolds the paper. Next, she staples a stack of 5½" x 8½" writing paper inside the cover and refolds the project. Lastly, she cuts out ears and facial features from construction paper scraps and glues them to the front cover of her journal as shown. Set aside time each day for students to write in their bunny journals. If desired, incorporate the following bunny-related prompts into your repertoire of writing activities:

- Write a tall tale about a bunny called Big Foot.
- Write a story about a bunny that can't hop.
- Describe three tricks you might teach a pet bunny.
- Writing from a bunny's point of view, tell how to find the juiciest carrot in a garden.

New Egg Unearthed

"Eggs-tra! Eggs-tra!" Read all about it! An egg like no other egg has been discovered! Will it hatch into an exotic reptile, an amphibian, an insect, or a bird? Is it the perfect ingredient for a delectable dessert? Can it be used to prevent bad breath, baldness, or backaches? Your students must decide! Have each child fold a 12" x 18" sheet of drawing paper in half and then cut through both thicknesses, trimming the paper into a desired egg shape. After he decorates the resulting booklet covers as desired, he trims writing paper to fit inside the covers and staples it in place. Then he writes about the exciting egg discovery in his booklet. Be sure to set aside time for these tales to be told!

Boxing Shell

The boxing shell is a very safe shell. It is shaped like a boxing glove. The shell is thick and hard. It is brown like mud and sort of ugly. This is good because people don't pick it up. If the animal inside the shell gets scared, sharp spines shoot out of the shell!

A Shell Showing

Big or small, smooth or spiny, vivid or plain, durable or fragile—shell homes vary a lot! Yet they are similar too, in that each shell home provides shelter and protection. Use a shell book to show the class a variety of shells. Point out physical and structural differences among the shells. Have students speculate about the pros and cons of different shell types, such as two-part shells, colorful shells, and heavy shells. Then challenge each child to design a state-of-the-art shell for a very lucky critter. Ask him to illustrate his shell creation on drawing paper and then name his shell and describe its physical features and benefits on writing paper. Be sure to schedule a shell showing so that each student can introduce the shell home he has created!

Sea Star Statements

How do sea stars affect the environment? Some sea stars feed off of coral reefs. Too much of this can damage the reefs. Sea stars also consume large numbers of oysters, clams, and scallops. On the other hand, sea stars remove harmful predators from oyster beds and reduce the amount of dead and decaying organisms in the world's saltwater habitats. For an engaging writing activity, have each child write an opinion statement about the environmental effects of sea stars and then support the statement with two or more facts. Be sure to set aside time for students to share their work!

I think sea stars are friends of the environment. They eat some things that are harmful. They also eat dead stuff, and that makes the ocean a cleaner place.

Jelly Beans in Space

Jelly beans in outer space? It's true! In June 1983 the space shuttle *Challenger* orbited Earth with two firsts on board—jelly beans and America's first female astronaut, Sally Ride. Share this fascinating fact with students; then have them brainstorm places jelly beans have probably never been, such as inside a volcano, a shark's stomach, or a pyramid. After each child traces a large jelly bean shape on story paper and cuts out the resulting shape, have him write and illustrate a story that describes the day he takes a bag of jelly beans to an unusual location. Have each child mount his completed story on a 9" x 12" sheet of colorful construction paper and then trim the paper to create an eye-catching border. After each child shares his far-out tale with the class, bind the projects into a class book titled "Jelly Bean Firsts" for further reading pleasure.

Seed Packet Pattern

Use with "Extraordinary Seeds" on page 52.

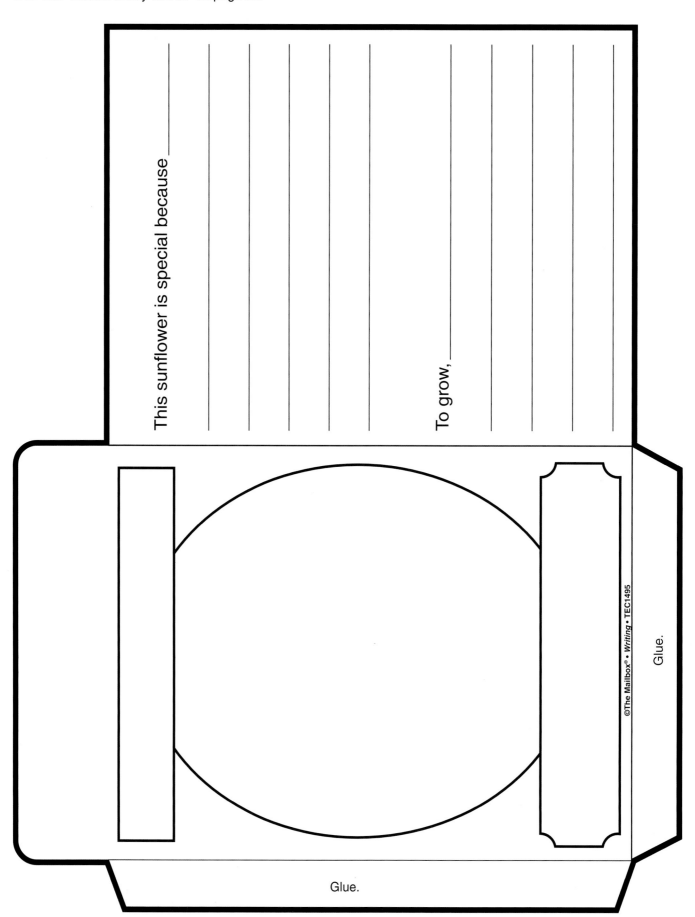

This sunflower is special because _____

To grow, _____

Glue.

Glue.

©The Mailbox® • *Writing* • TEC1495

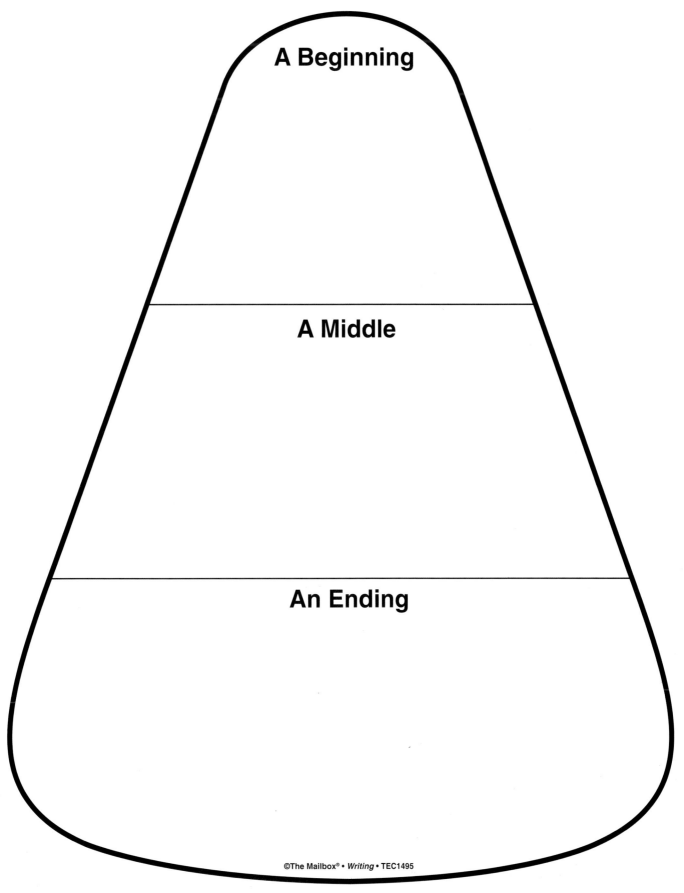

A Beginning

A Middle

An Ending

Shamrock Pattern
Use with "Special Shamrocks" on page 56.

I feel lucky to know you!

To

From

Learning Centers

The Mystery Box

A touch of suspense can magically perfect your youngsters' writing skills! Place a large gift-wrapped box with a removable lid, a supply of paper strips, a pencil, and an eraser at a center. Before the students arrive on Monday morning, place an object inside the gift-wrapped box and post one clue about its identity. (If desired, secure the box lid with a length of ribbon.) Each day, post an additional clue at the center. Students visit the center daily. When a student thinks he can identify the contents of the box, he writes his guess on a personalized paper strip and then deposits his guess in a designated container. On Friday reveal the mystery object. Each student who submitted a correct guess wins a small prize such as a sticker, bookmark, or pencil. What's the catch? Only those guesses that are written in **correctly capitalized and punctuated sentences** will be considered. No peeking 'til Friday!

Dianne Knight—Gr. 2, Frank C. Whitely School, Hoffman Estates, IL

It runs on tracks.

I think the mystery object is a toy train because a train runs on tracks.

Juanita

David Young

Oct. 20, 2005

Dear David,
 I was so excited to draw your name! I think you are the best. I loved the joke you told....

Special Delivery

Deliver year-round **letter-writing** practice at this versatile center. Write your students' names on individual slips of paper; then deposit the papers in a decorated container. Place the container, a supply of lined paper or stationery, an assortment of writing instruments, and a letter receptacle at a center. Also display a colorful poster that shows the parts of a friendly letter. To complete the center, a student draws the name of a classmate from the container and writes the classmate a letter. Then he places his completed letter in the letter receptacle and discards the paper slip. When each child has visited the center—and the container of student names is empty—ask a student or two to deliver the student-written letters. On his second center visit, a student writes a letter to the classmate who wrote to him. Once these letters have been delivered, restock the decorated container with student names and begin the letter-writing process again. In no time your youngsters' letter-writing skills will be in top form!

Mauri A. Capps—Grs. 1–2, Northlake Elementary, Dallas, TX

State-of-the-Art Sentences

Students can show their stuff again and again at this **sentence-writing** center! Use a colorful marker to label several craft sticks with nouns. Place the color-coded sticks in a container labeled "Nouns." Repeat the procedure to create color-coded sets of verbs and adjectives. Store the containers of craft sticks along with story paper, pencils, and crayons at a center. A student chooses a stick from each container and then uses the words on the sticks to create a state-of-the-art sentence. After he has written the sentence on his paper, he returns the craft sticks to the appropriate containers and illustrates his sentence. Youngsters are sure to enjoy this hands-on approach to sentence writing. For added writing inspiration, post samples of the students' work at the center.

Michelle Wolfe—Gr. 1, Kennewick, WA

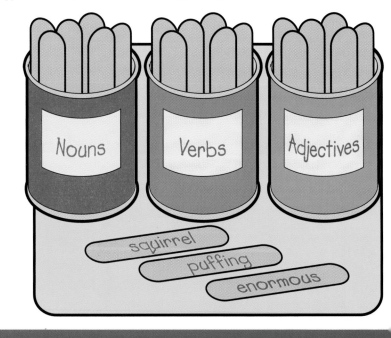

Nouns Verbs Adjectives

squirrel
puffing
enormous

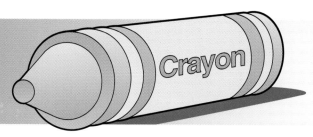

Colorful Character Sketches

Observation and imagination are key at this writing center! From old magazines or catalogs, cut pictures of five people who vary in age and appearance. Mount each picture on construction paper; then number the pictures and laminate them for durability. Also create a poster like the one shown that provides guidelines for writing a **character sketch.** Place the pictures, the poster, and a supply of writing paper at a center. A student chooses a picture and studies the person. Then he writes a brief paragraph that describes what he thinks this person is like. Encourage students to refer to the poster for writing ideas and tips. After completing his character sketch, he numbers his paper to correspond to the person he described.

When every student has completed the center, sort and post the paragraphs on a bulletin board near their corresponding pictures. Students are sure to enjoy reading the character sketches and comparing the different ways that each pictured person was described.

Maryann Chern Bannwart—Gr. 3, Antietam Elementary, Woodbridge, VA

Writing a Character Sketch

Think about these things:
- What does the person look like?
- What is his or her personality like?
- Where does the person live?
- What kinds of things does the person enjoy doing?

Remember these things:
- Be descriptive!
- Include interesting details!
- Write clearly!
- Be brief!
- Have fun!

Picture #1   Terrell

My character loves being outside. He lives in the northern part of the United States where it is cold in the winter. He enjoys bike riding, climbing mountains, camping, and hiking.

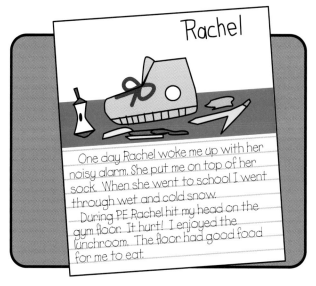

Rachel

One day Rachel woke me up with her noisy alarm. She put me on top of her sock. When she went to school I went through wet and cold snow.
During PE Rachel hit my head on the gym floor. It hurt! I enjoyed the lunchroom. The floor had good food for me to eat.

Sneaker Stories

Untying your students' creativity is a real "shoe-in" at this writing center. Place a supply of story paper and a shoebox containing crayons or markers at a center. A student slips off a shoe and sets it alongside her paper. Then she imagines life as that shoe. Next, she writes and illustrates a story from her shoe's **point of view.** Compile the students' work in a class book titled "Sneaker Stories" for further reading enjoyment. Now that's some fancy footwork!

Marge Schultz
Northside School
Fremont, NE

Silly Sentences

Reviewing parts of speech can lead to giggles and chuckles at this center! To make a silly-sentence booklet for each student, fold five sheets of blank paper into fourths as shown; then unfold the papers and staple them between two construction paper covers. Place the booklets, pencils, crayons, and scissors at a center. A student personalizes the cover of a booklet. Then, starting at the top of each blank page, he writes a four-word sentence—one word per section—in the following order: an adjective, a plural noun, a present-tense action verb, an adverb. When all five pages have been programmed, he cuts each page into fourths. To do this, he starts at the right margin of every page and cuts along each fold line until he is about one inch from the left margin. To read his booklet, the student randomly flips the strips and reads the resulting four-word sentences from top to bottom.

Cindy Marks—Gr. 3
Mark Twain Elementary School
Kirkland, WA

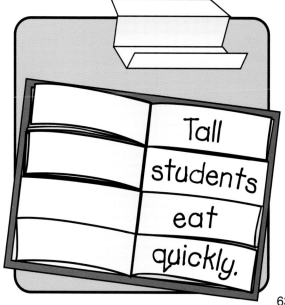

Tall
students
eat
quickly.

WANTED
JED T. TUCKER
jed t. tucker is wanted fur rustling cattle from the bucking bronco ranch. the cowpoke is also believed to have robbed miss kitty cooper last thursday at the silver spur store? he was last spotted near the town of wichita falls, texas. he is most likely headed for the state of oklahoma. sherrif sam slaney is offering a big reward to anyone who helps in the capture of Jed t. tucker.

"Spook-tacular" Stories

Creative writing is the focus of this center! Color a construction paper copy of page 69 and then laminate the paper. Next, cut out the cards and sort them into trick-or-treat bags labeled "Story Characters," "Story Actions (choose two)," and "Story Settings." Place the bags and story paper at a center. A student randomly removes one character card, one setting card, and two action cards from the bags. Then he writes and illustrates a corresponding story. When he is finished, he returns the cards to the bags. Invite students to revisit this center time and time again!

Rebecca Brudwick—Gr. 1
Hoover Elementary
North Mankato, MN

Proofreading Pals

Here's a partner center that clearly strengthens **proofreading skills**! On chart paper, write a paragraph that contains a predetermined number of mistakes like misspelled words and missing or inappropriate capital letters and punctuation marks. Display the paragraph—covered with clear acetate—at a center along with student directions, a dictionary, a corresponding answer key, several wipe-off markers, a container of baby wipes, and a trash can. A student pair proofreads the paragraph and uses wipe-off markers to make the necessary corrections. Once the edit is completed, the students check their work against the provided answer key; then they use a baby wipe to wipe the acetate clean so that the center is ready for another pair. Each week feature a different paragraph at the center. The message is clear—a proofreading center builds editing skills!

Sharon L. Brannan—Gr. 2, Holly Hill Elementary, Holly Hill, FL

bashful ghost

your school

flying

singing

A Bashful Ghost
There is a ghost at Hoover Elementary! It wants to learn to read. I see it flying in the library. Sometimes it is singing a song. I try to talk to it, but it flies away.

Write five tips for picking out a really cool pumpkin.

What if pumpkins could talk? Write a story about a talking pumpkin.

Last summer I lost a tooth. I put the tooth under my pillow. The next morning I found a pumpkin seed! At first I was mad. But then I got excited! What if the seed were magic? So I planted the seed right outside my bedroom window. You'll never guess what happened next! In only two days there was a pumpkin! It...

Pumpkin Tales

Harvest a crop of prizewinning writing at this seasonal center. Using a permanent marker, label four or five real pumpkins with different writing prompts. Display the pumpkins at a center along with crayons or markers and a supply of story paper. A student chooses a **writing prompt**; then he writes and illustrates a pumpkin story. No doubt these pumpkin stories will be the pick of the patch!

Tonya Byrd—Gr. 2
William H. Owen Elementary
Hope Mills, NC

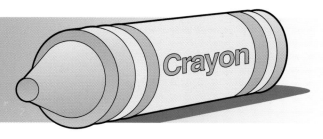

What's the Scoop?

Extra! Extra! Read all about it! At this writing center students write just-for-fun **newspaper articles.** Use a blue marker to label an envelope "Who?" and to write the names of several different people on individual paper strips. Place the color-coded strips in the envelope. In a similar manner create a color-coded envelope and a set of paper strips for each of the following questions: What? When? Where? Why? How? Store the envelopes, writing paper, and pencils at a center. A student selects a paper strip from each envelope and incorporates the information into a news story. After each student has completed the center, edit the stories and have each youngster write his final draft on a five-inch-wide strip of writing paper. If desired, provide blank paper for illustrations. Glue the students' work onto the pages of an old newspaper; then place this hot-off-the-press edition in your classroom library for all to read.

Mary Anne Murphy—Grs. 3–4
Andrew Jackson Language Academy
Chicago, IL

And the Time Is...

Time keeps on ticking at this math and **story-writing** center! Cut out a supply of individual comic strip frames that portray a variety of times. Store the frames at a center along with pencils, crayons, glue, 9" x 12" sheets of colorful construction paper, and copies of page 70. A student chooses a comic strip frame and glues it in the center of a horizontally positioned sheet of construction paper. After she determines when the illustrated event might have occurred, she completes a copy of page 70. Then she glues her completed work to the back of her construction paper.

To make a kid-pleasing class book, stack the students' work so the comic strip frames are faceup. Bind the pages between tagboard covers and title it "And the Time Is…" Place the book in the class library for hours of reading enjoyment.

Rosetta M. Sanders—Gr. 2, Zervas School, Newton, MA

Scheduling Time

Here's a kid-pleasing activity that integrates **telling time and writing.** Place a clock stamp, a stamp pad, pencils, crayons, and a supply of blank paper at a center. A student titles her paper "A Perfect Saturday" and then stamps a column of clockfaces down the left edge of the paper as shown. She programs the first clock to show the time she'll get out of bed. To the right of the clock she writes the matching analog time in crayon, and then she uses a pencil to describe what she plans to do at that time. She programs and labels the remaining clocks on her paper to show the activities she'd schedule for her perfect day. Display the completed schedules, and plenty of time-related conversations will follow!

Stacie Stone Davis
Lima, NY

Thank-You Notes

In honor of National Teacher Day (annually Tuesday of the first full week in May), ask students to write **thank-you notes** to their favorite educators. Place stationery or notecards, envelopes, and assorted writing instruments at a center. Also display a colorful poster that shows the parts of a thank-you note. A student selects a current or former teacher and pens a note of thanks to him or her that includes a memorable learning experience. Next, he labels an envelope with the teacher's name and seals his note inside. Have students hand-deliver their notes or assist them in preparing their notes for mailing—whichever is appropriate. These kindhearted messages will generate miles of smiles!

Leslie Bussey—Gr. 1
Millbrook Elementary School
Aiken, SC

Dear Ms. Bussey,
Thank you for being a great teacher. You have taught me lots of things this year. I really liked learning to read and write. I also liked learning about rocks. I had so much fun at the rock mine. I like you very much!
Love,
Jake

Writing Treasure

Yo-ho-ho! There's a booty of **creative-writing** inspiration at this center! Decorate a box (with a removable lid) so that it resembles a treasure chest. Place the chest, story paper, pencils, crayons, and a student dictionary at a center. Each week stock the chest with four or five items that will encourage creative writing. A student removes the items from the chest, and then he writes and illustrates a story that is inspired by them. If desired, compile each week's stories into a class book titled "Weekly Writing Treasures From [date]."

Ruthie Jamieson Titus—Gr. 3
Union Elementary
Poland, OH

The Magic Biscuit

Once upon a time a dog ate a very yummy biscuit. It was...

Surprising Stories

These story bags are packed with writing inspiration! Gather picture cards from an old Memory game or make picture cards by attaching stickers to tagboard squares. Then, for each picture card, program a corresponding word card. Laminate all the cards. In each of several resealable plastic bags, sort four picture cards and their matching word cards. Store the resulting story bags, pencils, and a supply of paper at a center. A student chooses a story bag and matches each picture card to a word card. Then she **writes a story** that includes the four pictured items. Just imagine the surprising stories that will result!

Beth Jones—Gr. 2, Stevensville Public School
Stevensville, Ontario, Canada

Raindrops Keep Falling on My Head!

Integrate science and language arts with this **poetry** center. Cut large raindrop shapes from light blue construction paper. Place the cutouts, glue, silver glitter, and a supply of white paper (precut to fit inside a raindrop) at a center. A student writes a weather poem on a piece of white paper; then he glues his poem onto a raindrop cutout. As a finishing touch, the student adds a border of silver glitter around his raindrop. Post the glittery raindrop poems under a large cloud that students have covered with cotton balls. Now that's a display that's perfect for any kind of weather!

Kristy Bowling—Gr. 3
Sky View Elementary School, Mableton, GA

This dog loves to snorkel. It will swim right next to you. It can even fetch shells underwater. This dog would be fun to have as a pet.

Pick a Pet

Your animal lovers will find this **paragraph-writing** center especially appealing. Cut an assortment of animal pictures from old magazines. Place the cutouts and a supply of writing and construction paper at a center. After choosing a picture, a student writes a paragraph in which he describes the animal and explains why it would make a terrific pet. Then he mounts the picture and his paragraph on construction paper and trims the construction paper to create an eye-catching border. Display the completed projects on a bulletin board titled "Pick a Pet."

adapted from an idea by Leigh Anne Newsom—Gr. 3
Greenbrier Intermediate
Chesapeake, VA

Photo Album Fun

Make **descriptive writing** a personal matter with this writing activity. Have each youngster bring a photograph from home that can be included in a class photo album. At a center, place a photo album containing a supply of 8½" x 11" self-adhesive pages and a supply of writing paper. Also post a list of questions such as the ones shown. Using the posted questions as a guide, a student writes a descriptive paragraph about his snapshot. Then he attaches the photograph and his paragraph to a blank album page. When each student has completed the center, place the album in your classroom library for all to enjoy.

Rachelle Dawson—Gr. 3
Nashua School
Kansas City, MO

WHO is in the picture?

WHERE was the picture taken?

WHAT was happening in the picture?

WHEN was the picture taken?

WHY did you choose to bring this picture to school?

My dog Sofie loves to eat. Here she is begging at a picnic we had last summer. I think she is sweet.

Invent a Pet!

Unleash your youngsters' **creative writing** at this one-of-a-kind center! Enlist your students' help in creating a list of pets. Place the resulting list at a center, along with a supply of story paper, pencils, and crayons or markers. A student invents a new kind of pet by combining two pet names. She writes the name of her unique pet on a sheet of story paper; then she illustrates the pet and writes about its unique abilities. Compile the pet-related projects in a class book for further reading enjoyment!

Laura Horowitz—Gr. 2
Embassy Creek Elementary
Cooper City, FL

Pet List

kitten	ferret
puppy	canary
iguana	parakeet
horse	tarantula
rabbit	parrot
snake	llama
goldfish	guinea pig
turtle	hermit crab
hamster	
gerbil	
lizard	

Parabit
A parabit is very cool because it hops around like a rabbit and it sings like a parakeet. It can fly too. A parabit is also very smart. It can learn tricks.

Wanted: Perfect Summer

All-day cartoons, daily trip to the playground, hot dog or hamburger lunch, ice cream daily at 3:00, 2 hours of swimming, weekly trips to the movies. Call 123-4567.

Wanted: Perfect Summer

Put your youngsters' writing skills to the test when you ask them to pen **classified ads** for the perfect summer! Read aloud several classified ads and discuss with students the kinds of information included in the ads. If desired, also read aloud your local paper's guidelines for writing these ads. Place several samples of classified ads, a supply of writing paper, and pencils at a center. A student writes a brief ad seeking the perfect summer. After each student has completed the center and the ads have been edited, have each student copy his ad on a two-inch-wide paper strip. Mount the ads on blank paper to resemble pages from the classifieds; then make a class supply for students to read over the summer.

adapted from an idea by Tammy Brinkman and Kimberly Martin
San Antonio, TX

Picture-Perfect Memories

Use the photos you've taken during the school year at this **personal narrative writing** center! Place the snapshots, pencils, crayons or markers, clear tape, a stapler, and half sheets of writing and construction paper at a center. A student selects a photo, describes her memory of the pictured event on writing paper, and staples her writing between two pieces of construction paper. Then she tapes the photo to the front cover and adds a title, her name, and other desired decorations. Now that's a picture-perfect memory!

Alyce Pearl Smith—Gr. 1
Butzbach Elementary
Butzbach, Germany

Parent Night
by Mandy Tercel

silly spider	laughing	spooky house
bashful ghost	crying	dark, damp forest
brave pumpkin	shaking	your school
friendly bat	eating	a pumpkin patch
	flying	
	running	
	singing	
	searching	

70 Name _____

Got the Time?

Think about the event pictured in the cartoon.
Write the time the event happened on the clock and in the speech bubble.
Write a story about the event.

Note to the teacher: Use with "And the Time Is..." on page 65.

Write On!

Ideas and Tips for Teaching Students to Write!

By Gum, It's Magic!

Youngsters can really sink their teeth into this **creative-writing** activity. To begin, show your youngsters a supply of individually wrapped pieces of sugarless gum. Explain that when it's chewed, this gum can cause their imaginations to run wild! Suggest to your youngsters that they might imagine themselves shrinking to the size of mice, growing as large as dinosaurs, or sprouting wings to fly. Distribute the gum, and ask each youngster to write and illustrate a story about her chewing gum adventure. Compile the completed stories into a class booklet titled "By Gum, It's Magic!"

Beth Jones—Grs. 1–2, General Vanier School, Niagara Falls, Ontario, Canada

Critter Zoo

Create extraordinary writing enthusiasm with a collection of stuffed critters! Label an area of your classroom "The Critter Zoo," and place an assortment of stuffed animals and several writing journals (one per critter) at the location. After establishing a checkout procedure, invite students to take the critters and journals home. Encourage youngsters to include the critters in their normal afterschool or weekend activities. Then instruct the youngsters to write **stories** in the journals about their critters' visits. When the pages of a journal become filled, replace the journal cover with a student-illustrated booklet cover and place the resulting booklet in your classroom library for all to enjoy.

Tanya Wilder—Gr. 3, Wolf Creek Elementary, Broken Arrow, OK

Pass the Book

Students will be eager to complete this appealing homework activity! You will need a construction paper booklet that includes one blank page of writing paper per student, a stuffed animal, and a cloth or plastic bag. To introduce the activity, have students agree upon a name for the stuffed animal; then label the booklet cover "The Adventures of [animal's name]." Place the booklet and the stuffed toy in the bag. Each night, assign a different student to carry the bag home and write an **adventure story** on a booklet page. When each student has written a story, display the completed booklet along with the stuffed animal in your classroom library for your youngsters' reading enjoyment. If desired, continue the activity throughout the year by using an assortment of stuffed toys.

Rita Peat—Gr. 3, Cleveland Elementary, Elkhart, IN

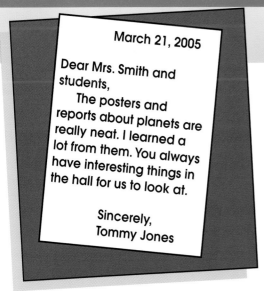

March 21, 2005

Dear Mrs. Smith and students,

The posters and reports about planets are really neat. I learned a lot from them. You always have interesting things in the hall for us to look at.

Sincerely,
Tommy Jones

Letters of Praise

The backdrop for this **letter-writing** activity is your school's hallways! With your students in tow, visit each school hallway display. Take time to carefully examine the student-made pictures, reports, and projects on exhibit. When all of the displays have been visited, return to the classroom and list them on the board. Next, have students choose their favorite displays, making certain that each display has been chosen by at least one student. Then, in letters written to the appropriate teachers (and their students), have your youngsters express what they liked about the displays. Your students will enjoy writing such important letters, and the recipients of the letters will be thrilled to learn that their work is being admired by others.

Julie S. Polak—Grs. 1–2, North School, Galion, OH

Percy is my pet porcupine. My uncle gave him to me. He is still a baby. He likes to eat carrots. He sits in my lap when we watch TV. When he grows up, he will protect me from bullies. Percy is my perfect pet!
by Trysten

Pet Paragraphs

Paragraph writing is easy to "purr-fect" when pictures of possible pets provide writing inspiration! Each student selects a pet by cutting out a picture of an animal from an old magazine. As a prewriting activity, he names the pet and lists details about it. Then he uses his ideas to write a paragraph about his new pet. To assemble his work, he glues his cutout and paragraph on construction paper as shown. Bind completed projects into a class book titled "Perfect Pets and Paragraphs!"

adapted from an idea by Diane B. Rinehard—Gr. 2, Beechgrove Elementary, Independence, KY

A Watermelon Is...
by Deon

Mouthwatering Descriptions

Here's a **descriptive-writing** activity that your youngsters can really sink their teeth into! Display a large uncut watermelon. On white bulletin board paper, sketch a colorful outline of a large watermelon slice. Display the resulting poster. After each child has studied and felt the actual fruit, have students brainstorm words that describe how the melon looks and feels. Record these words on the poster. Next, give each youngster a small slice of watermelon on a paper plate. As students sample the fruit, have them brainstorm words that describe how it smells and tastes. Add these words to the poster. In conclusion, have each student compose a mouthwatering description of a watermelon titled "A Watermelon Is..." If desired, have students write their paragraphs in student-made watermelon booklets like the one shown.

Carol Gibb—Gr. 1, East Elementary School, Menomonie, WI

Shadow and the Witch

Once upon a time there was a ⚲ who had a black 🐈 named Shadow. She and her 🐈 lived in an old house that had many 🕷s and 👻s in it.

Every Halloween the ⚲ opened her house to the people in town for a party. She and her 🐈 carved many 🎃s and put them out by the barn where the ⚲ lived.

Creative Writing With Confetti

This spellbinding writing activity is sure to enchant your youngsters! Purchase a supply of holiday-shaped confetti. Introduce each confetti shape and write its name on the board. Encourage students to refer to the resulting word bank as they write **seasonal stories**. Then have each student copy her completed story on a blank sheet of paper, gluing confetti shapes in place of the corresponding words. Invite students to share their tales aloud; then bind these remarkable rebus stories into an eye-catching book.

Carol Ann Liske—Gr. 3, Betty Adams Elementary School, Westminster, CO

I see a spooky little ghost.
He is sitting on our fence post.

by Annie

Creepy Couplets

Make writing time hauntingly fun with "spider-ific" **couplets!** To begin, post a student-generated list of Halloween words. Give each student a 3" x 5" index card and ask her to write a couplet (two lines of rhyming poetry) that includes one or more words from the list. Next, have each child make a construction paper spider. To do so, she glues a three-inch and an eight-inch circle together. She adds eight accordion-folded paper strips for legs, two wiggle eyes, and a construction paper mouth. Then she glues her couplet on her spider project. To showcase your students' work, tack a web of yarn on a bulletin board. Add the poetic arachnids and title the display "Creepy Couplets."

adapted from an idea by Rebecca Brudwick—Gr. 1, Hoover Elementary, North Mankato, MN

Liozebiraffe

Creative Creature Writing

Zebras with giraffe necks and mice that roar may be just what your youngsters are looking for! Enhance **creative writing** by reading aloud the book *You Look Ridiculous Said the Rhinoceros to the Hippopotamus* by Bernard Waber. In this story a hippopotamus decides he wants to change his appearance. The results are literally laughable. At the conclusion of the book, challenge youngsters to blend the body parts of various animals to make new creatures. Have each student draw, name, and write about his creature. Suggest that each child include information about his creature's habitat, food preference, personality, and interests. Display the creations on a bulletin board titled "Really Ridiculous Creatures," or bind them into a class book. These creatures may not be real, but the skills your students gain from this exercise will be!

Gina Parisi—Gr. 2, Demarest Elementary School, Bloomfield, NJ

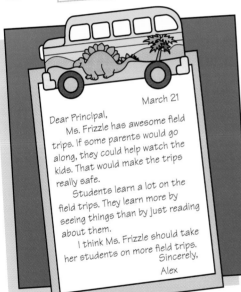

We're Thankful for...

Boost your students' self-esteem with this **creative-writing** activity. Pair students and ask each student to interview his partner. Suggest that students ask their partners about their strengths, favorite school subjects, hobbies, and family members. When the interviewing process is complete, have each student write a story about his interviewee on a piece of seasonal writing paper. Next, have each student color a cornucopia pattern and then glue a picture of his interviewee on the cornucopia. Mount each cornucopia and story on a sheet of construction paper. Staple the resulting projects to a bulletin board titled "We're Thankful for Our Classmates."

Debbie Sherrill—Gr. 2, Orange Hunt Elementary, Springfield, VA

On the Road With Ms. Frizzle

Deliver a kid-pleasing **persuasive-writing** experience with the help of the Friz! Read aloud one or more books from Joanna Cole's Magic School Bus series. Then ask students to suppose that the principal at Ms. Frizzle's school has refused to let her take any more field trips because he thinks they are dangerous. Ask each youngster to write a persuasive letter to try to change the principal's mind. Then have him decorate a small bus cutout to resemble the Magic School Bus and glue it on a sheet of construction paper with his letter. Display students' work on a bulletin board titled "Dear Principal."

Debbie Erickson—Grs. 2–3 Multiage, Waterloo Elementary, Waterloo, WI

Wacky Weather

There's no shortage of food or fun in Judi Barrett's outrageous weather-related story *Cloudy With a Chance of Meatballs*. After reading this story to your students, challenge them to write **comical weather reports** for other fictitious towns. Each report should include several weather predictions that involve foods and beverages. Since no weather report is complete without a station identification, suggest that each student name a radio or television station as the source of her report. Set aside time for students to read their reports to their classmates. Your classroom will be more fun than the land of Chewandswallow!

Patti Hirsh—Gr. 3, Casis Elementary, Austin, TX

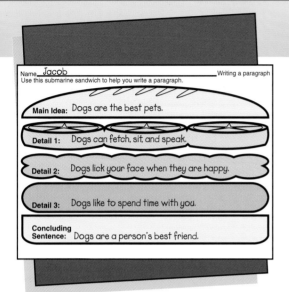

Name __Jacob__   Writing a paragraph
Use this submarine sandwich to help you write a paragraph.

Main Idea: Dogs are the best pets.

Detail 1: Dogs can fetch, sit, and speak.

Detail 2: Dogs lick your face when they are happy.

Detail 3: Dogs like to spend time with you.

Concluding Sentence: Dogs are a person's best friend.

A "Sub-stantial" Organizer

Watch your students sink their teeth into writing with this "sub-stantial" **paragraph organizer!** On a piece of poster board or chart paper, create a submarine sandwich similar to the one shown. Refer to the sandwich chart as you teach your students how to organize and write a paragraph. Next, provide a copy of page 87 for each child. Direct students to write a paragraph on a given topic by completing their sheets and then transferring the ideas to another piece of paper. Encourage students to organize a paragraph in the same manner every time they are given a new topic. Youngsters' appetites for writing are sure to grow with every new paragraph!

adapted from an idea by Maureen M. Casazza, Honesdale, PA

The best holiday season I remember is the year we went to Disneyland. I saw Mickey Mouse. He looked like Santa. His dog Pluto looked like a reindeer. It was fun!

"Holly-day" Happenings

Create an adorable "holly-day" display with this **story-writing** idea! Draw a large holly leaf on white paper, add writing lines, and duplicate one holly leaf for every student. Provide an assortment of story starters, such as "My favorite thing about December is..." and "The best holiday season I remember is..." Have each child select a story starter and write a story on his leaf. Then have the student cut out his holly leaf, glue it onto a slightly larger piece of green construction paper, and trim the green paper to create an eye-catching border. Arrange the completed cutouts on a wall or bulletin board in the shape of a giant wreath. Add a few red paper berries and a big red paper bow for a colorful display!

Loretta W. Lombardi—Gr. 3, Mercer Christian Academy, Trenton, NJ

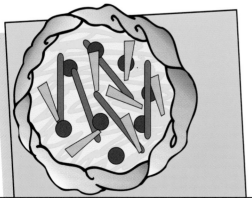

Jessica likes grapes, carrots, licorice, and lemon pudding on her pizza.

Pizza With Pizzazz!

Any way you slice it, this tasty activity teaches students how to use **commas in a series!** Write a student-generated list of favorite foods. Then write a silly pizza-related sentence on the board that lists four favorite foods as toppings. For example, you might write "Hope likes ice cream, strawberries, spaghetti, and cream corn on her pizza." Explain that when a sentence contains a list of three or more items, commas are used to separate the items in the list. Ask each child to write several sentences that list silly pizza toppings. Then have her copy her favorite one on provided paper and use construction paper scraps, glue, and crayons to decorate a brown paper circle to resemble the pizza she described. For a 3-D crust, she rolls brown paper towels and glues them around the edge of her pizza. Display the projects with the title "Pizzas With Pizzazz!"

Sharon L. Brannan—Gr. 2, Holly Hill Elementary, Holly Hill, FL

Who Said It's January?

The sky did when it
sent a flurry of snow.

The mittens did when
they got ready to be worn.

The icicle did when it
formed outside our house.

The carrot did when it
became a snowman's nose.

The fireplace did
when its fire cracked
and popped.

Sue

My goldfish is very patriotic. He has
a shiny red tail. His top fin is bright
blue. He has white dots on his body.
His name is Uncle Sam.

The Case of the
Missing Candy Bar

Every day this week Manny's candy bar was missing from his lunch.
Each time, he found a paper clip in
its place. Manny began asking questions. He paid one nickel to each
person who could give him a clue.

Who Said It's January?

Reinforce the concept of seasonal changes with this **poetry** idea. Begin with a discussion of the sights, sounds, and events of January. Make a list of students' observations. On a length of bulletin board paper, write the title "Who Said It's January?" Model the style of the poem by writing the first line as an answer to the question. Ask children to create additional lines for the poem, designating a narrator for each line. Write each student's contribution on the bulletin board paper. Conclude the poem with the lines "Who said it's January? Now you know!" If desired, have students add seasonal cutouts to the poem before you display it for all to enjoy.

Patricia E. Buob—Grs. 1–2 Multiage, Central Road School, Rolling Meadows, IL

Flamboyant Fish

Reel in some great **descriptive writing** with this splashy activity! Give each student a fish cutout to decorate. To promote creativity, provide a variety of decorating supplies, such as crayons, markers, glitter, sequins, paint pens, and scraps of wallpaper and fabric. Next, ask each student to write a descriptive paragraph about her flamboyant fish. Collect the paragraphs and the fish; then display the fish in a prominent classroom location. Read each paragraph aloud and invite students to determine which fish from the display is being described. Students will quickly realize the importance of descriptive details and may be anxious to try this activity again. Perhaps creating and then describing striking seashells would be in order?

Diane Vogel—Gr. 3, W. B. Redding School, Lizella, GA

Whodunit?

Turn your students into supersleuths with this **mystery-writing** activity. To set the mood, read aloud a favorite mystery story. At the conclusion of the story, write a mystery title like "The Case of the Missing Candy Bar" or a writing prompt like "It was a warm spring day when our teacher mysteriously disappeared during math class" on the board. Then divide the class into small groups and give each group a clear plastic bag that contains three unrelated objects, such as a paper clip, a nickel, and a plastic comb. Challenge each group to determine how each of the three objects in its bag could be used to help solve the mystery at hand. Then have each student write and illustrate his version of the story on story paper, or have the students alternate writing sentences for a group story. Be sure to set aside time for the students to share their work with their classmates. No doubt this activity will have everyone asking, "Whodunit?"

Carol Ann Perks—Grs. K–5 Gifted, Comstock Elementary, Miami, FL

My Mom Is Smart
I wanted to go to Ben's house. My mom said I could go if my room was clean. I promised my brother a quarter if he would put my clothes away. He even found the green sock I lost last week! My dog ate all the crumbs on the floor plus a plastic ring and a toothpick. I gave him a dog bone. At first my mom was very happy. Then she looked under the bed. I hope I get to go to Ben's next Saturday!

Silly Shari set sail for Sweden with six salami sandwiches and seven strawberry sodas.

To Mom
Lots of Love,
Rodney

May 7, 2006

Mom, you are special to me because you make pancakes on Saturday morning!

It's in the Bag!

Adding a touch of mystery to your next **creative-writing** lesson is sure to produce intriguing results. The day before the writing activity is to be completed, give each child a paper lunch bag to take home with instructions to return the bag the following school day with five small items inside. Tell students that the contents of their bags should remain a secret. For the writing activity, challenge each child to pen a story that incorporates the five items in his bag. Next, have each student read his story aloud. At the end of each reading, invite the class to guess which five items from the story are in the writer's bag. When a correct guess is made, have the writer remove the item from his bag. If the five items are not guessed in five tries, the writer has outsleuthed his audience! Repeat this activity as often as desired. Clever writers and excellent listeners are sure to follow.

Maryann Chern Bannwart—Gr. 3, Antietam Elementary, Woodbridge, VA

Entertaining Tongue Twisters

What could be more fun for students than **writing tongue twisters?** How about writing tongue twisters about themselves? To set the stage for this activity, read aloud assorted tongue twisters from a book such as *Six Sick Sheep: 101 Tongue Twisters* by Joanna Cole and Stephanie Calmenson. Then challenge students to pen several personalized tongue twisters. Next, ask each child to choose her favorite twister to copy and illustrate on provided paper. Invite students to share their silly sentences with the classs. Then collect the projects and compile them into a book titled "Several Silly Students." This tongue twister collection will quickly become a class favorite!

Catherine V. Herber—Gr. 1, Washington Elementary, Raleigh, NC

A Gift From the Heart

Begin this special **writing project** a few weeks before Mother's Day and each child will have a loving gift for his mother or another loved one. For a two-week writing project give each child ten 4" x 6" sheets of drawing paper inside a quart-size resealable plastic bag. For each of the next ten school days, have every child remove one blank booklet page from his zippered bag and then copy, complete, and illustrate a sentence like "[Name], you are special to me because…" Ask students to store their completed pages in their plastic bags. When all ten pages are written, have each child select a sample of wallpaper from which to make his cover. Cut a 7" x 9" rectangle from the wallpaper sample, fold the cutout in half, and staple the student's pages inside. If desired, have each child use a permanent marker to personalize and date the front inside cover of his booklet. The recipients of these loving keepsakes are sure to be thrilled!

Jeannette Freeman—Gr. 3, Baldwin School of Puerto Rico, Guaynabo, Puerto Rico

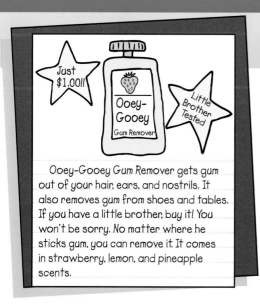

Making the Sale

You won't have to sell this **creative-writing** activity to your students—they'll be thrilled to write and illustrate advertisements! First, have students contemplate the impact that magazine and television advertisements have on the purchases that they (and their families) make. Next, invite students to name different ways that companies get consumers interested in their products. Then challenge each child to write and illustrate an ad for a brand-new product. Require that each ad contain the name of the product being sold, a description of it, a reason for buying it, and an illustration of it. Set aside time for each youngster to pitch her new product to the class!

Julie Simpson—Gr. 2, Cherry Elementary School, Toledo, OH

Three-Part Autobiography

The end of the school year is the perfect time for students to recall the past, describe the present, and plan for the future. On the board write "When I was younger I…," "Now I can…," and "When I am older I…" Have each child copy and complete each phrase on a different 4½" x 5" rectangle of writing paper. Next, have her fold a 12" x 18" sheet of light-colored construction paper into thirds, unfold her paper, and glue her writing in chronological order at the bottom of the paper (using the crease lines as guides). To complete her three-part **autobiography,** she writes her name in large letters near the top of the project and illustrates each writing sample in the remaining space. Display the completed projects for all to read!

Eve Bell—Gr. 2, Hershey Elementary, Lafayette, IN

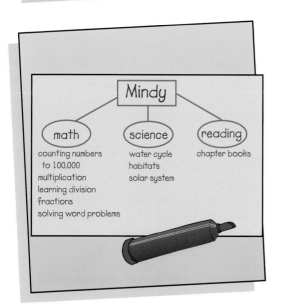

The Art of Persuasion

Expect an enthusiastic response when you present this end-of-the-year writing challenge. Ask students to imagine that the school principal has announced that he will promote only those students who can prove they are ready for the next grade level! Have each child draw a web like the one shown, write her name in the rectangle, and in each oval name a subject she's shown growth in during the past school year. Below each oval have her list specific things she learned in that subject. Then direct each child to write a letter to the principal that will convince him to promote her. Encourage each student to incorporate the main ideas and supporting details from her web into her very **persuasive letter.**

Nicole Weber—Grs. 2–3, Waterloo Elementary School, Waterloo, WI

Butterflies in My Belly

If you're looking for a way to set your students' **personal narrative–writing skills** aflutter, try this! As a class, discuss the meaning of the saying "I have butterflies in my stomach." Then ask students to talk about times they have felt butterflies in their stomachs and to describe the events that provoked these feelings. Next, give story paper and two butterfly stickers to each student. Ask each youngster to illustrate herself and attach the butterfly stickers to the stomach of her artistic likeness. Then have each student write about an event that caused her to get butterflies. Encourage students to share their completed projects. Knowing that butterflies find their way into lots of bellies can be comforting to your students.

Anne Culberth, Nixa Espy Elementary, Nixa, MO

Twigatops

My dinosaur discovery is the Twigatops. He is very nice. He eats lots of grass. He looks like a big fat bush. I wish I had a Twigatops in my backyard. That would be very cool.
by Gene W.

"Invent-a-saurus"

Looking for some "dino-mite" writing inspiration? Try this! Have each child cut out a tagboard dinosaur pattern. Then have him take home his cutout and invent a new type of dinosaur by decorating the cutout with a chosen item. For example, a Cottonasaurus might be covered with cotton, a Twigatops adorned with twigs, and a Stamposaurus rex embellished with canceled stamps. Set a date for the dinosaur projects to be returned. Then schedule writing time for students to pen **paragraphs** about their prehistoric creatures. Display the completed projects together on a bulletin board titled "Priceless Prehistoric Discoveries!"

Mary E. Maurer, Caddo, OK

Lost in the Leaves!

Clues
★ 1. It is bigger than a quarter.
★ 2. It is smaller than a pancake.
★ 3. You cannot eat it.
★ 4. It is a toy.
★ 5. It has string in the middle.

Lost in the Leaves!

"Be-leaf" it or not, students' **sentence-writing skills** begin piling up during this activity! Each child chooses an object that could be lost or hidden in a pile of leaves. Then, keeping the object's identity a secret, he writes five clues about it on a 9" x 12" sheet of drawing paper. As the students write, move around the classroom reading their sentences. Star each complete sentence and leave a fall-colored leaf pattern for the writer. When a child collects five leaf patterns, he cuts out each one. Next, he turns over his paper and illustrates his mystery object near the center of the blank page. Then he lays his leaf cutouts, one by one, atop his illustration, taping only the stem of each leaf to his paper (see the illustration). He also titles his work. Have each child, in turn, hold his project so that his classmates can view the leaf pile and he can read aloud his clues. After reading each clue, he entertains two guesses. If his mystery object isn't identified, he folds back one leaf. He continues until the hidden object is identified or revealed.

Anne Hott, Washington County School, Hagerstown, MD

In a Nutshell

This nutty idea is a memorable way to introduce the concept of **summarizing!** Display an acorn (or a picture of one). Tell students that the acorn gives a hint about what the expression "in a nutshell" means. Invite students to speculate about the meaning of the phrase. Then lead them to conclude that it means "in just a few words." Explain that when a person summarizes, he tells about main points very briefly, or in a nutshell. Next, give each student a sheet of writing paper and two 9" x 12" sheets of construction paper. Also provide access to a stapler and an acorn-shaped template that is approximately 7" x 9". The student uses the materials to make a one-page booklet like the one shown. He summarizes a favorite story inside the booklet. Then he titles and decorates the booklet cover. There you have it—summarizing in a nutshell!

Todd Helms—Gr. 2, Pinehurst Elementary, Pinehurst, NC

Award-Winning Books

Each year the American Library Association awards the Caldecott Medal to the illustrator(s) of the book it considers to be the most outstanding picture book of the preceding year. Past winners of this award have been the illustrators of *The Polar Express, Owl Moon,* and *Grandfather's Journey.* Share several Caldecott Medal–winning books with your students and discuss their outstanding features. As a follow-up **paragraph-writing** activity, have each student select a picture book that he feels is worthy of a similar award and write a paragraph about the book. Each paragraph should include the book's title, its author and illustrator, a description of the artwork, and reasons the student feels this book should earn an award. If desired, have students design construction paper awards that can be paper-clipped to the chosen books. Compile the written projects into a book titled "The Best Picture Books: A Classroom Guide." Display the award-winning books and the student-published guide in your classroom library.

Nancy Wojcik—Gr. 2, Hayes Elementary School, Kennesaw, GA

Take Note!

Introductions are in order with this **paragraph-writing** activity! By student vote, select a school staff member whom the class would like to know better. Help students compile a list of interview questions; then arrange for the staff member to visit the class. Have volunteers interview the guest as the remaining students take notes. Conclude the interview with refreshments, such as cookies and punch.

After the guest's departure, enlist students' help to create a web that shows the information gathered (see the illustration). Point out that the web provides a handy reference of main ideas and details. Then ask each student to use the web to write two or more well-organized paragraphs. Not only will students improve their writing skills, but they will also become better acquainted with a staff member!

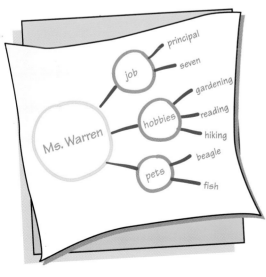

Ruthie Jamieson Titus—Gr. 3, Union Elementary, Poland, OH

Sweet to My Senses!

Mix America's favorite flavor with this activity on using **sensory words in writing** and what do you get? A lesson that's a sweet treat! Give each student a peanut butter cup pattern like the one shown. The student traces the pattern on five sheets of notebook paper, cuts out the tracings, and staples them behind the pattern. Then she labels each blank page with one of these verbs: *tastes, smells, feels, looks,* and *sounds.* Next, give each student a small Reese's peanut butter cup. At your signal, the child places the candy in her mouth and slowly eats it. As she eats, she lists descriptive words for the candy on her booklet pages. When everyone is finished, have students share their words and use the resulting word banks to write paragraphs about the sweet snack.

Bette J. Mattox—Gr. 3, San Jose Episcopal School, Jacksonville, FL

Once-Upon-a-Time Stories

For a timely **creative-writing** booklet that's loads of fun, try this! Ask each child to select a main story character from a list of animals. (For the best results, limit your list to animals that are easy to portray on paper plate covers like the one shown: frog, mouse, bear, pig, bunny, dog, cat, etc.) To make his cover, a student traces a flattened paper plate onto an appropriate color of construction paper, then cuts out the circle and glues it to the plate. Next, he uses colorful paper, markers or crayons, a brad, precut hour and minute hands, glue, and scissors to create an animated clock-face that resembles the main character of his story.

Using his cover for inspiration, a student writes a once-upon-a-time tale on provided booklet pages. Encourage students to give their main characters names and to include several time-related references in their stories. When a student's story is complete, he flips over his cover and staples his story, in sequential order, to the back of the cover. As each child takes a turn reading his story aloud for his classmates, have him manipulate the clock hands on the cover to coincide with the story events. Wow! Time *does* fly when you're having fun!

Mary Ann Lewis, Tallahassee, FL

Colorful Comparisons

This tasty approach to **writing similes** ensures sweet success! On the board tape one circle cutout in each of the following colors: brown, blue, orange, red, green, yellow. Also give each child a handful of M&M's candies. As the students munch on their candies, ask them to brainstorm similes for each color of circle. Then have each student make a step booklet like the one shown. First, a student draws a line that is 2½ inches from one end of her brown rectangle (see the paper list below); then she folds the paper on the line. Next, she slides the remaining rectangles into her booklet cover to create graduated layers and staples the resulting booklet near the fold. On each booklet page, a student writes one or more similes that correspond to its color; then she personalizes and decorates the booklet and cover as desired.

Construction Paper Needed for Each Booklet		
All colors are 4½" wide.		
brown: 9½" long	**orange:** 4" long	**green:** 5½" long
blue: 3¼" long	**red:** 4¾" long	**yellow:** 6¼" long

Candy Whelan—Gr. 3, Garlough Elementary, West St. Paul, MN

My Silly Clown
My clown has curly orange hair and two pink ears. His yellow nose is big and round. He is grinning because he just drank a big glass of milk. Some of the milk is still on his face. His hat and collar are green and purple. His hat is small and has circles on it. His collar is big and striped. He looks silly!

Red

Red is
A juicy apple,
Rudolph's nose,
Tomato soup,
And my face when I cry.

Red is
My favorite shirt,
A stoplight,
My first bike,
And a rose that smells really good.

That is what red is to me.
by Mira Stovall

Nicholas

Sweet As Sweet Potato Pie
My grandma loves me a lot. I love her a lot too. I like it when she tells me I am sweet as sweet potato pie. One day she was sick. I made her a card. Then I picked her some flowers. They were the little ones that grow in her yard. She hugged me tight. She told me I was as sweet as sweet potato pie!

One-of-a-Kind Clowns

Do you believe that clowning around can enhance **descriptive writing?** You will at the conclusion of this activity! Have each child complete a copy of page 88. Encourage him to color his clown creatively and list four descriptive words for each clown part. Then provide plenty of time for students to write their paragraphs. For a fun follow-up, collect the students' completed papers. Tape the clown portraits to the board and then read the paragraphs to the class. Ask a different child to match each description to a clown. No funny business here, just descriptive writing at its best!

Susan M. Stires—Gr. 3, Sam Houston Elementary, Wichita Falls, TX

Colorful Poetry

To introduce this **poetry-writing activity,** give each child a sheet of paper and a colorful marker (crayon or colored pencil). Ask her to think about the color of her marker and then use it to list phrases that describe the feelings, ideas, or objects she associates with its color. Next, use student-contributed phrases to write a color poem like the one shown for the class. Then instruct each student to pen an original color poem using phrases from her brainstorming. To publish her poem, she mounts her final draft on construction paper in the color of her poem topic. Showcase the projects on a bulletin board titled "Colorful Poetry."

Sue Lorey, Arlington Heights, IL

Sweet Stories for Mom

Mem Fox's well-loved picture book *Koala Lou* provides the inspiration for this **story-writing** activity. As you read aloud this story of a mother koala and her cub, place special emphasis on the mother koala's refrain: "Koala Lou, I DO love you!" Next, ask each child to think of a sweet expression that he likes to hear his mother (or another significant woman) say to him. Then have him write and illustrate a story that incorporates the expression he chose. Explain that the story can describe a special time that has already happened or one that he hopes will happen. Moms are sure to cherish these Mother's Day surprises.

Marsha Portnoy—Grs. K–5 Reading, Village Elementary School, Syosset, NY

Superlative Sentences

Inspire students to **write out-of-the-ordinary sentences** with this unique activity! On the board list five or six simple sentences like "A castle appeared" and "A lion roared." Ask each student to illustrate one of the displayed sentences on a 12" x 18" sheet of paper. Encourage students to create detailed scenes. After a given amount of time, ask each child to write a sentence on a one-inch-wide paper strip that tells about her illustration. Next, challenge students to add more details to their sentences. To do this a child writes the words she wishes to add to her sentence on a second one-inch-wide paper strip. She cuts these words apart and then cuts her original sentence apart so that she can insert the additional words. Invite students to repeat this editing process until they are satisfied with their sentences. Then have each child glue her sentence to her illustration. Be sure to set aside time for students to share their superlative work!

Geraldine Gutowski, Sombra del Monte School, Albuquerque, NM

Story Chain

A **story chain** is a wonderful technique in which students can cooperatively practice their writing skills. Read a story to your class and ask students to think of a sequel to the story. Give an index card to each student. Choose one student to create a beginning sentence for the story sequel and write it on his index card. Call on another student to create the second sentence and write it on his card. Continue in this manner until everyone has contributed a sentence. Then have each student illustrate the sentence on his index card. Punch two holes in each card as shown; then use yarn to link the cards together in sequential order. Attach a title card to the beginning of the story. Display the resulting story chain where students can enjoy reading their work.

Suzanne Kulp—Gr. 2, The Harrisburg Academy, Wormleysburg, PA

Very Healthy Caterpillars

Reinforce good eating habits with this literature-based writing activity. Read aloud *The Very Hungry Caterpillar* by Eric Carle and lead students to conclude that the insect gets a stomachache because it is not eating healthful foods! Then have students **write original versions of the story** in which the caterpillar eats a well-balanced meal. To begin, a student stacks her white construction paper (see the paper list) to create graduated layers; then she staples this paper between her green paper to create a step booklet. On the front cover, she writes her name and the title "The Very Healthy Caterpillar." Next, she illustrates the caterpillar and a nutritious food on each booklet page, making sure the size of the caterpillar increases on each page. Then she labels and hole-punches each food item. On the back of the last page, she illustrates a gorgeous butterfly. To complete the project, the student writes a beginning and an ending for her story (on separate strips of writing paper) and glues the writing inside the front and back booklet covers. Spectacular!

Lisa Plackner—Gr. 2, Westside Elementary, River Falls, WI

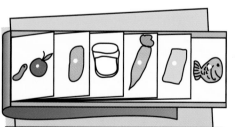

Paper Needed for Each Booklet
writing paper: two 3" x 9" strips
construction paper: 4½" wide
    green: two 12-inch lengths
    white: 2" long, 4" long, 6" long,
             8" long, 10" long, 12" long

Eddie
I am lovable!
I am a good friend.
I am nice to animals.
I smile a lot.
I am very helpful.
Yes! I am lovable!

Precious Poetry

This **poetry-writing activity** is sure to boost the self-esteem of your young writers. To set the stage, read aloud *The Lovables in the Kingdom of Self-Esteem* by Diane Loomans. Encourage students to recall positive qualities of the book's animal characters. Then ask each child to list on scrap paper several of his own positive qualities. To begin his poem, he writes his name as the title and the sentence "I am lovable!" as the first line. For each of the next five (or more) lines of his poem, he writes a brief sentence that describes one positive quality about himself. He concludes his poem with the line "Yes! I am lovable!" After each child decorates his work, publish the poems in a class volume titled "The Lovables in Room ___."

Maureen Burke Iannacone—Gr. 1, Enfield Elementary, Oreland, PA

My animal is gray. It has four legs. Its skin is wrinkled. Its ears are big! It has a very long trunk. It has a short tail that swishes back and forth.

Circus Critters

Looking to strengthen **descriptive-writing skills?** This circus-related project is sure to do the trick! Write a list of student-suggested circus animals on the board. Have each child secretly select one animal from the list and then, without revealing the animal's identity, write a description of it on a 2" x 9" strip of yellow construction paper. Next, she folds a 9" x 12" sheet of white construction paper in half (to 6" x 9"). Keeping the fold at the top, she unfolds the paper and illustrates on the bottom half the animal she described. She uses crayons to decorate the front of the folded paper to resemble an old-fashioned circus wagon. Then she glues her description to the top edge of the wagon (trimming it as desired) and two construction paper wheels to the bottom edge. For an interactive display, showcase the projects with the title "The Circus Is in Town!" Challenge students to read each description, decide which animal is described, and then peek inside the project to check her answer.

Doris Hautala, Washington Elementary School, Ely, MN

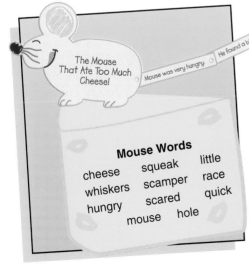

The Mouse That Ate Too Much Cheese!

Mouse was very hungry. He found a big hunk of cheese. He ate and ate and ate. Mouse ate too much. He could not get in his mouse hole!

Mouse Words

cheese   squeak   little
whiskers   scamper   race
hungry   scared   quick
mouse   hole

A Tail With a Tale!

Students will scurry to write **complete sentences** for this adorable project! On yellow paper trimmed to resemble a cheese wedge, list mice-related words suggested by your students. Next, give each child a full-page mouse pattern and three or more 1½" x 9" paper strips. A child writes a story title on his mouse pattern, decorates the mouse, and cuts it out. Then he authors his mouse story, writing each sentence on a different paper strip. (Ask students to leave a one-inch margin at both ends of every strip.) After he edits his sentences for beginning capitalization and ending punctuation, he arranges them in story order. Next, he uses brads to assemble his project as shown. Then, starting with the last sentence, he slides each strip under the previous strip. He continues until the entire mouse tail is tucked from view. Now *his* mouse tale is ready to be told!

Candy Wendorff—Gr. 1, Lake Asbury Elementary, Orange Park, FL

First, twist the top cookie off.

Tasty Task

What's sandwiched between two Oreo cookies? Creme filling and a tempting opportunity to **write directions!** Post a class-generated list of transition words. Explain that the words are handy for giving directions. To demonstrate, give every student one Oreo cookie and access to a supply of white paper circles. As each youngster eats her cookie, she uses appropriate transition words to write each step of the process on a separate circle. Then she sequences the circles and staples them between two black construction paper circles. After the youngster uses a white paint pen to title the resulting booklet, she trades the booklet with a partner. She uses her partner's directions to eat a second cookie and then she gives her partner feedback about the clarity of the directions. Delicious!

Kimberly Wannall—Grs. 3–4, Acclaim Academy, Davidson, NC

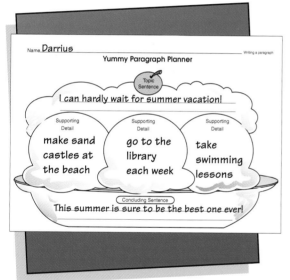

Cool Summer Plans

Who knew that **writing a paragraph** about summer could be such a tasty experience? First, ask students to speculate how they'll spend their summer break. Suggest that they consider daily activities as well as special family outings. Next, give each child a copy of page 89. As a class, review the parts of a paragraph. Then ask each child to organize his summer-related thoughts on the page before he writes his paragraph on writing paper. Invite interested students to share their writing with the class. Encourage every child to display his writing on his family's refrigerator for a cool reminder of his summer plans!

Reba Cross—Gr. 3, Alpine Elementary, Alpine, TX

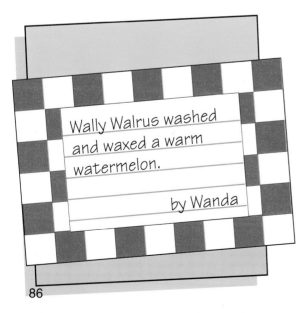

Wally Walrus washed and waxed a warm watermelon.

by Wanda

Tasty Tongue Twisters

This serving of **alliteration** becomes a fun-to-read class book. On the board write a student-generated list of picnic foods whose names begin with consonant sounds. Have each child write on her paper one food from the list, circle the word, and then write other words that have the same initial sound as the circled word. Challenge each child to use words from her alliterative list to write silly tongue twisters. Next, have each student publish her favorite tongue twister. To do this, she copies the sentence on a 4" x 6" rectangle of writing paper, colors a 6" x 9" rectangle of graph paper to resemble a checkered tablecloth, and then mounts her writing on the colored page. Bind the students' pages into a class book titled "A Tongue Twister Picnic!"

adapted from an idea by Lisa Morris, LaGrange, GA

Use this submarine sandwich to help you write a paragraph.

Main Idea:

Detail 1:

Detail 2:

Detail 3:

Concluding Sentence:

Note to the teacher: Use with "A 'Sub-stantial' Organizer" on page 76.

A One-of-a-Kind Clown

Color the clown.
Study each clown part listed below.
On the lines, write words that tell about it.

hat _____

hair _____

nose _____

ears _____

mouth _____

collar _____

Use a sheet of writing paper.
Write a paragraph that describes the clown.
Be sure to use some of the words you listed!

©The Mailbox® • *Writing* • TEC1495

Note to the teacher: Use with "One-of-a-Kind Clowns" on page 83.

Yummy Paragraph Planner

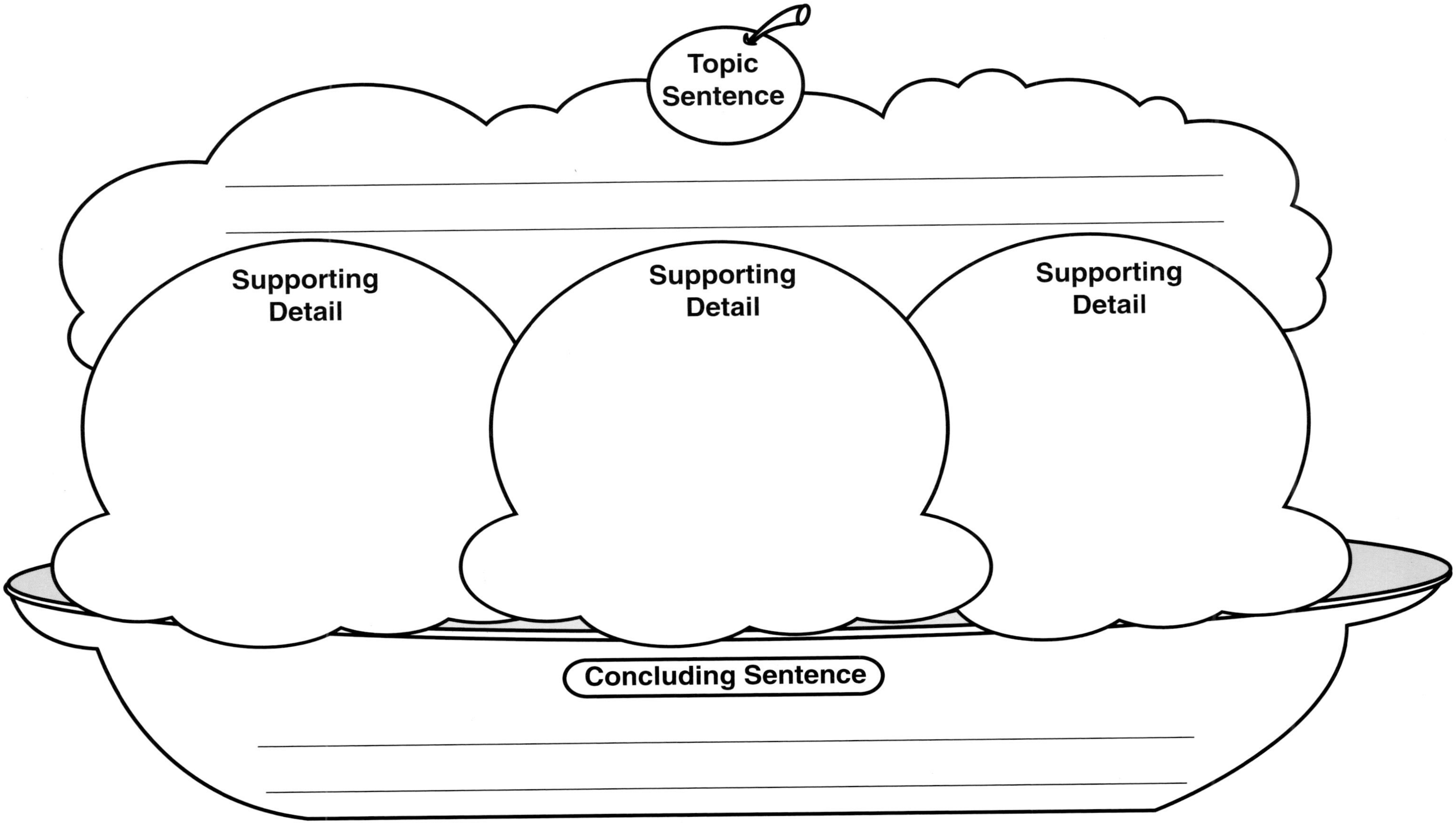

Topic
Sentence

Supporting
Detail

Supporting
Detail

Supporting
Detail

Concluding Sentence

Note to the teacher: Use with "Cool Summer Plans" on page 86.

Our Readers ► Write

WRITING TIPS FROM TEACHERS

Charting a Writing Course

If **keeping track of your students' writing projects** leaves you feeling shipwrecked, try using a chart like the one shown. Laminate the chart for durability and have each student record her progress with a dry-erase marker. A quick glance shows you at which stage each student is working. When a student completes her project, she wipes away her marks.

Kelli Casper
Rockport Heights Elementary
Arnold, MO

Name	Rough Draft	Conference	Edit	Peer Review	Final Copy	Illustrate	Publish
Angela	✓	✓					
Brandon	✓	✓	✓				
Chelsey	✓						
Damon	✓						
Emil	✓	✓					

Writing to Go

To encourage students to practice **writing stories and letters** at home, pack some nifty writing supplies in a briefcase. Include supplies such as colorful envelopes and writing paper, drawing paper, and an assortment of pencils, markers, and erasers. Each student will eagerly await his turn to take the briefcase home.

Sue Gramling
Hodge Elementary
Denton, TX

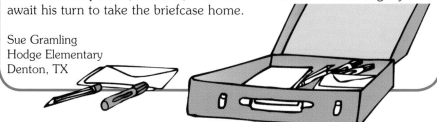

Glorious Get-Well Greetings

With this **writing project,** sending a get-well greeting becomes a big-book learning experience. When a child has an extended illness, have her classmates dictate a special story for her. First, have the students choose a favorite storybook character, such as Ms. Frizzle. Then have the youngsters dictate a story about this character visiting the sick child. In the letter encourage students to include information about the things they have been learning in school. When the story is completed, copy it onto large booklet pages that have been cut in a desired shape. Have the students illustrate the booklet pages and a booklet cover; then staple the pages behind the cover. Deliver the student-made project to the youngster.

Debbie Anderson—Gr. 1
Costa Catholic School, Galesburg, IL

Ms. Frizzle Visits Julia

Teacher's Journal

Nothing thrills a student more than a personal note from the teacher. Keep a bound notebook exclusively for written correspondence between teacher and students. Each day, write a short letter to one student in your class. At the end of the day, let that student take home the journal and write her response on the next page. If desired, respond to the student's letter before writing a new letter to the next student. Make sure all students have participated before starting over again. Not only will your students receive real-life practice with **letter writing,** but they'll also enjoy learning more about you and their classmates.

Nancy Steen—Gr. 2
Floyd Elementary School
Mesquite, TX

Dear Ms. Steen,

Dear Brittany,
I read about your win in last week's skating tournament. I'm very proud of you! I've never been a great ice-skater, so maybe you can give me some tips.

Family Business Letters

When teaching your children to write **business letters,** try this activity. Obtain each parent's workplace address (secretly if possible). Then have students write letters to their parents requesting information about their businesses. Parents will be delighted to receive these letters, and the students will benefit from the business information they receive. In cases of unemployment, arrange for children to write to businesses that they find especially interesting.

Ritsa Tassopoulos—Gr. 3
Oakdale Elementary, Cincinnati, OH

End-of-the-Year Keepsakes

Students and parents will be delighted with the results of this end-of-the-year keepsake project. Give each child a half sheet of paper with space for an illustration and manuscript lines. Have him write a few **sentences** about his favorite school memories and then draw a picture to resemble himself in the space provided. Photocopy pairs of student pages side by side on single sheets of paper; then duplicate each full page for each student. Have each student place his pages between two construction paper covers and then decorate his front cover as desired. No doubt these books will really be treasured.

Karen Brighton Gesl—Gr. 2
Indian Head Elementary
Indian Head, MD

My favorite memory of second grade was when we hatched chicks from eggs.

Kyle Beck

My favorite memory was when our class got the most points at Field Day.

Jacob Prillaman

Bag-It Booklets

These booklets provide a **protective covering** for your youngsters' creative work. Gather a supply of resealable plastic bags. Using a hole puncher, punch identical holes in the left-hand margin for each bag. Also precut a supply of paper to fit inside the bags. A student writes and illustrates a story on the precut paper. Then, keeping his story pages in order, he slides each page (or every two pages, back-to-back) inside a plastic bag. Next, he aligns the holes and uses lengths of yarn to tie the individual bags together. His completed booklet is ready for display. Later, the story and lengths of yarn can be removed, and the bags are ready to be used again.

Rebecca L. Gibson
Auburn, AL

Journal Newsletters

Weekly student-written newsletters are a perfect way to keep parents informed! Ask each family to provide a spiral notebook for this purpose. Every Friday, spend time with the class reviewing the past week. Also preview upcoming events of the next week. Then, in her notebook, each child writes a letter to her family in which she describes her accomplishments of the week and mentions upcoming events. Ask each family to write in the journal a response to the weekly letter. Students love the ongoing correspondence with their parents, and parents appreciate the chance to observe their children's progress from week to week.

Wendi Sumner—Gr. 3, Mill Plain Elementary, Vancouver, WA

Letterman

When you're ready to teach your youngsters about **writing personal letters,** let Letterman lead the way! Make a large poster of Letterman as illustrated. For Letterman's body, give an actual example of a friendly letter. When introducing Letterman to your class, talk in a robotic monotone just for fun. Your students won't soon forget Letterman or the help he gives to improve writing skills.

Donna Bridges—Gr. 2
Glenwood School
West Plains, MO

"All About My Teacher" Class Book

Have students collectively make this end-of-the-year class book for a treasured keepsake. Supply each child with a sheet of paper. Have him write one or two **paragraphs** telling something about you and his favorite experiences in your class; then have him illustrate his page. Next, have him write your name vertically on the back of his paper and use each letter to start a word or phrase that describes you. Bind all students' pages together between construction paper covers and title the book "All About My Teacher." This special book will be not only a wonderful memento but also a great icebreaker to share at next year's open house.

Laura Sunley
Powell, OH

Parent-Child Response Journals

Periodically use **parent-child response journals** to extend the self-discovery writing process and enhance parent-child communication. On the board write one journal topic designed for the student and one for the parent. Each child responds to the student topic, records the parent topic in his journal, and takes the journal home so that his parent can respond to the appropriate topic. Encourage each parent to discuss his journal response with his child before sending the journal back to school. Some parent-child topics that you might use include the following: The most important lesson my parent (child) taught me…, If I could do anything differently…, The way I would describe my family (child)… Your students will learn as much about themselves as they will about writing.

The most important lesson my parents taught me was to share. Now my friends share with me.

The most important lesson my child taught me…

Pamela M. Szegedy, Erieview Elementary School, Avon Lake, OH

Author on Tour

Official Book Tour

Each time an author in your classroom **publishes a story,** arrange for the student to take her latest book on tour. Determine a tour date; then schedule brief appointments with the school principal, the school nurse, a former teacher, and other school staff for that day. On the day of the tour, clip an official-looking badge like the one shown to the young author's clothing and give her a list of her scheduled tour stops. Each staff member who hears the youngster's story writes a brief comment and signs the back cover of her book. You can bet your students will keep publishing their stories right up to the very last day of school!

Susan Bunte—Grs. K–3
Crest Hills Year-Round School, Cincinnati, OH

Daily Reflections

Conclude each school day on a positive note! Every week distribute student copies of a **daily reflection chart** like the one shown. At the end of each day have every child write on his chart what went well that day and a goal for improvement. Sign each student's chart and add a note as desired. Ask each child to have his parent sign the chart and return it the following day. Parents are sure to appreciate the positive communications and, as an added bonus, you'll have detailed records for anecdotal notes.

Natalie Foster—Grs. 2–3, The Discovery School
Gambrills, MD

Daily Reflections by _Scott_				
For the Week of _January 14–18_				
	What went well?	How can I improve?	Teacher	Parent
Mon.	I did really well on my spelling pretest.	I will listen carefully to directions.	Great job on the pretest! Remember your math homework! Ms. Foster Ü	
Tues.				

Paper Pen Pal

Your youngsters will be involved in this **letter-writing** activity in a few minutes flat. Read aloud *Flat Stanley* by Jeff Brown. In the story, Stanley—after being flattened—takes advantage of his slender physique by traveling to California in an envelope. To set the stage for a related activity, have each student create a construction paper likeness of Flat Stanley. Then ask each child to bring to school the address of a friend or relative who lives out of state. Next, have each student write a letter to his friend or relative. In his letter he introduces Stanley and requests that Stanley be returned, after a brief visit, with a letter explaining what Stanley did during his visit. Each student then addresses an envelope and places Stanley and his letter inside. When the envelopes are in the mail, title a bulletin board "Flat Stanley's Travels" and display a map of the United States there. As each child's Flat Stanley returns, have him find and mark on the map where Stanley has been; then read aloud the accompanying letter.

Nancy Conner—Gr. 2
Turnpoke Christian School
Grand Prairie, TX

Nov. 10, 2005

Dear Lashay,
I was happy to hear from you. Stanley came to school with me. He went with me at lunch. Mrs. Ives showed us the state of Texas.

Coffee Talk

Perk up your **journal-writing** sessions with this easy idea. Divide your students into small groups. Give each group a decorated coffee can in which you have placed strips of paper programmed with journal topics. Have one member from each group select a strip from the can and read aloud the topic. Then give each group a few minutes to brainstorm possible ideas and experiences relating to this topic. When talk time is over, each student begins writing about the topic in her journal. Chances are you won't hear a student complaining that she has nothing to write about!

Laurie Mounce—Gr. 2 Student Teacher
Bryan, TX

Journal Buddies

Who says **pen pals** have to live out of state or attend another school? Your students can form pen pal relationships right in their own school! Work with a teacher from a different grade level to set up a buddy system. Then provide each student with a buddy and a buddy journal. Explain to students that they will periodically swap journals with their pen pal buddies, so they should direct their written comments to them. The more frequently their journals are exchanged, the stronger the bonds will be between the writing partners. Look for opportunities to expand these relationships into other curriculum areas. Then culminate this writing project with an end-of-the-year picnic.

Pam Fleury—Gr. 3
Chamberlain Elementary
Chamberlain, SD

Research Journal

Motivate your students to learn about a variety of topics with this unique approach to research. Instead of each student taking the class mascot (stuffed animal) home and writing about something they did together, ask each student to research a topic to teach the mascot (and his classmates too). Challenge your students to use a variety of reference materials and then write what they learn in a class **research journal**. When each student returns the stuffed animal to school, have him share his journal entry with the class. What an exciting way to practice research skills as well as oral and written expression!

Holly Penhorwood—Gr. 3
St. Matthew School, Gahanna, OH

Rex's Research Journal

Month-by-Month Memories

Monthly memory albums are a great way to keep parents up-to-date with school-related happenings. Each month photograph a variety of activities. When the pictures are developed, give one snapshot to each child. Then, on provided paper, have each student **write a photo caption or paragraph** that describes the event. Place the completed projects in a three-ring binder or inexpensive photo album. Attach a class list and a brief parent note inside the front cover. When a child returns the album, he checks off his name on the class list and gives the album to the next student listed. After each child's family has seen the album, showcase it in the classroom library.

Phyllis Hoffmeister—Gr. 2
New Washington School
New Washington, IN

We went to Hill Ridge Farm. We went on a hayride and picked pumpkins.

Sweet Correspondence

This idea provides a sweet start for a **letter-writing** activity. Poll your students to find out their favorite candy snacks. List the candy names on the board, along with the companies that make them. Then ask each student to write a friendly letter to the company that makes his favorite kind of candy. Each child should tell why he likes the candy so much. He may also request a free sample of the candy if desired. When each child's letter is complete, he addresses an envelope to the respective company (a company's address can be found on its product's wrapper) and places his letter inside. With hopes of sweet samples for their efforts, students will be eager to pick up their pencils and write friendly letters.

Katherine V. Gartner—Special Education Grs. 1–2
Oxhead Road Elementary School, Centereach, NY

Holiday Postcards

Reinforce student **writing skills** by turning old holiday cards into festive postcards! Round up a supply of cards; then cut off the back portion of each one. Use a pen to draw lines on the back of each resulting postcard as shown. Challenge students to write and address postcards to their family members. For added fun, provide an assortment of holiday stickers for students to use as postage stamps. Encourage students to hand-deliver their completed postcards. What a great way to recycle holiday cards and practice writing skills!

Carolyn Hill
Richland Elementary
Richland, MI

Journals in a Jiffy

These **mini journals** are a snap to make! To make a journal, stack several half sheets of blank paper atop a length of wallpaper or gift wrap that you've cut to the same size. Fold the stack of papers in half so that the decorated paper becomes the journal cover and the blank paper becomes its pages. To bind the journal, securely tie a length of string elastic around the fold. For added fun, customize the covers of the journals to complement the season or a current teaching theme. You can count on plenty of writing enthusiasm as students record their thoughts in these unique mini journals.

Candy Whelan—Gr. 3
Garlough Elementary
West St. Paul, MN

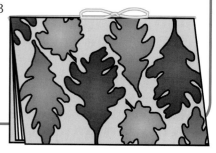

Easy Edits

Looking for an easier way to **edit students' writing?** Try this helpful method. Gather a supply of green-and-white, lined computer paper. Have students write their rough drafts on this paper—using only the white lines. Remind students of this rule with the phrase "Write on the white." When the rough drafts are done, edit students' papers by writing in the green space above each writing line. As students write or type their final drafts, they can easily see the corrections or suggestions that you've made. Now you've got the "write" idea!

Sharon L. Brannan—Gr. 2
Holly Hill Elementary
Holly Hill, FL

Bone-Chilling Stories

Send chills up your students' spines with this small-group **writing** activity! First, have each group brainstorm spooky words and write them on a large bone-shaped cutout. Next, ask each group to share five words from its cutout. Encourage the other groups to add these words to their collections if appropriate. Then have each group write a scary story that includes ten spooky words from its cutout. After each group has shared its work with the class, mount each story and its corresponding bone cutout on a bulletin board titled "Bone-Chilling Tales!"

Jill Hamilton—Gr. 1
Schoeneck Elementary, Stevens, PA

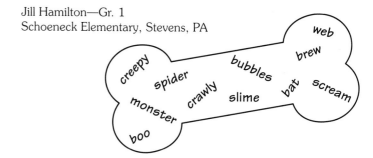

Thanksgiving Letters

Recipients of these **student-written letters** will be thrilled! Before Thanksgiving, ask each child to select a person for whom he is very thankful. Then, in a friendly letter written to this person, the student explains why he appreciates the person so much. Have each child decorate an envelope with Thanksgiving artwork and then slip the final copy of his letter inside. Suggest that each child hand-deliver his letter on Thanksgiving Day, or have him enlist the help of a parent in sending the letter to its lucky recipient.

Ruth Heller—Gr. 3, Public School 156, Laurelton, NY

Miniature Booklets

If your film processor gives you a small photo album free of charge each time you have film developed, this tip is for you! Cut paper to fit each sleeve in the album. Then have students use the precut paper to design **booklet pages** of any type. Slip the pages into the album sleeves—back-to-back, if desired. To reuse the album at a later date, remove the programmed pages and slip in a newly designed set.

Theresa Fleming—Gr. 1
Robert Gray Elementary
Aberdeen, WA

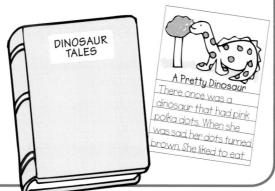

Jelly Bean Poems

Since spring and jelly beans go hand in hand, why not make jelly beans the focus of a springtime **poetry project?** After a lesson on similes, introduce the format of the jelly bean poem shown. Give each child a sampling of different-colored jelly beans and let the writing begin. Mmm! Poetry is positively delicious!

Candy Whelan—Gr. 3
Garlough Elementary
West St. Paul, MN

> ### Jelly Beans
> *by Maggie Holter*
>
> Jelly beans are...
> As red as apples,
> As green as trees,
> As purple as violets,
> As yellow as bees.

Read All About It!

Extra! Extra! Here's a great way to review the events of each school day and ensure that students can answer the often asked question "What did you do in school today?" At the end of each day, write student-dictated sentences about the day's events on story paper. Have a volunteer illustrate and date the page before posting it in the room. At the end of the month, gather all the daily news reports and glue them on folded sheets of bulletin board paper or newsprint to resemble a **newspaper.** Add a front-page headline. Students love being able to read this newspaper in their spare time. Second-language learners may also find that reading this paper helps them become familiar with the past tense of many words.

Julie Bradley—Gr. 1
Santa Cruz Cooperative School
Santa Cruz, Bolivia

Shapely Journals

This tip for making **student journals** is a cut above! To make a journal, tear a sheet from a desired seasonal or theme-shaped notepad and staple it atop a stack of blank or lined paper. Trim around the shaped paper and the journal is ready to use!

Jodi Schrick—Title 1 Reading
West Lyon Elementary School
Rock Rapids, IA

Work in Process

For those times when you wish to **display students' stories** and other written projects that have not been edited and/or rewritten, take this approach. Post a sign that reads "Temporary Spelling" or "First Drafts." This helps children feel a sense of accomplishment without feeling as though every composition has to be perfect to be appreciated. And this approach also shares your objective with other students and adults who stop to admire the students' work.

Marlene Trissell
Ginnings Elementary
Denton, TX

A Recipe for a Mom

Cook up a wonderful Mother's Day gift with this **recipe-writing** activity! To familiarize students with recipe ingredients and cooking instructions, read aloud several cooking recipes. Next, brainstorm with the class ingredients that could be included in a recipe for a super mom. Also discuss possible cooking directions. Then use the students' ideas to write a recipe for a super mom on the board. Instruct each child to carefully copy the recipe onto a large recipe (or lined index) card. Laminate the cards; then have each child glue a silk flower or attach a colorful sticker to her project. Now that's a recipe every mom will love!

Recipe: Super Mom
From: Sharron
story for sleep
2 bags of kindness
barrel of caring
million buckets of stories
teaspoon of strictness

Pour all of the ingredients into a cozy house. Keep them safe. All of these ingredients make a loving, caring, and protecting mom.

Bonnie Hemstad—Gr. 2
Baxter Elementary
Baxter, MN

Father's Day Fix-It Book

Fathers—and other significant males in your students' lives—will wonder what they ever did without these helpful, **humorous home-repair guides.** Ask each child to think of several things that have needed repair around her home and choose one to write about. Have each child write a complete description of how her chosen repair can be (or was) made. Photocopy each repair description and a booklet cover for each of your students. Staple the covers and pages into booklets; then send a booklet home with each child. This gift may not be very helpful for quick fixes around the house, but it's just the right tool for giving dads' spirits an extraordinary lift!

Fixing a Flat

First, you take all that stuff out of the trunk. Then you pump up the can. Next, you borrow Bobby's dad's jack. You spin it round and round. Now you pump down the can and you're done!

by Sherry

Lisa Marram—Gr. 1
Glendale, CA

Journal Illustrations

Give daily **journal writing** a new twist! Start by giving each youngster (and yourself) a journal of blank story-writing paper. Each day write in your journal while students write in theirs. Rather than illustrate your own writing, end each writing session by selecting one child to add illustrations to your entry. It's a great opportunity for students to showcase their comprehension skills and artistic talents. And as an added bonus, they get to know their teacher better too. There's little doubt that your journal will quickly become the most-read and best-illustrated volume in the classroom!

Last night I went to see my dad. I told him about our accident yesterday with the math manipulatives. He laughed so hard he almost fell out of his wheelchair!

Linda Stec—Gr. 3
Deford Elementary School, Deford, MI

Ms. Jackson is going to be a zookeeper. She will work with the tigers and the owls. She will tame a bear.

Oh, the Places You Will Go!

If your class was assisted by a student teacher, thank her for all her efforts with this **class booklet.** After sharing *Oh, the Places You'll Go!* by Dr. Seuss, ask each youngster to name a different place he thinks your student teacher will go after graduation. Have him write and then illustrate a few sentences about this place. Collect these pages; then bind them between two construction paper covers. Write the title "Oh, the Places [student teacher's name] Will Go!" on the front cover. Present the booklet to your student teacher on her last day as a special memento.

Denise Lapine—Gr. 2
Tracey Laszlo—Gr. 2
Rockwell Elementary School, Nedrow, NY

Time for TAG

How do you teach students to **peer-edit** properly? Try the TAG approach. At the end of a writing session, pair students. Have each child carefully read what his partner has written. Then provide time for each child to do the following: Tell his partner what he likes about his writing. Ask his partner questions about his writing. Give his partner suggestions for improving his writing. In no time at all, your youngsters will be giving positive critiques of their classmates' writing, and their written work will prove it!

Kimberly Hofstetter
Oakland County School District
Bloomfield Hills, MI

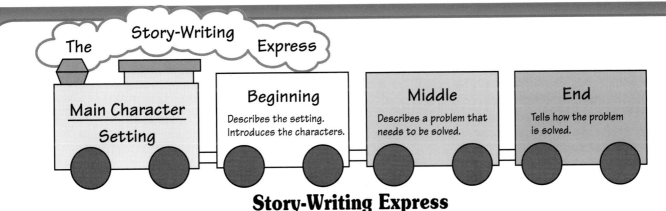

Story-Writing Express

Keep students on the "write" track with a locomotive spotlighting **beginning story-writing elements.** Prepare or purchase tagboard cutouts of an engine and three train cars. Program the cutouts as shown. Introduce and display the engine first, explaining that a main character and a story setting must be chosen before a story can get rolling. Then display the three train cars in sequential order, explaining each story part as you go. Encourage students to refer to the locomotive whenever they write stories. All aboard the Story-Writing Express!

Pat Urbach—Gr. 1, B. A. Kennedy Elementary, Prairie du Chien, WI

Cookbook for Mom

Cooking up this **one-of-a-kind cookbook** is a laugh a minute! Each child writes a recipe for the most delicious food his mom (or another significant person in his life) makes. Type the completed recipes and make a class set of each one. Then collate the copies and bind them into individual books that students can give their moms. A good laugh will be had by all!

Alice Bertels—Special Education
Crestview Elementary, Topeka, KS

Fresh-As-Spring Writing Samples

Just in time for warm spring breezes, create a **clothesline display** for students to air their finest writing. Secure a length of string or cord beneath your chalkboard ledge and place a basket of spring-type clothespins nearby. If a student wishes to display a sample of his writing, he clips it to the clothesline using a couple of clothespins. To keep the display fresh, encourage students to routinely replace their own writing samples. Then invite students to hang out at the display and read what their classmates have written.

Deb Jacobson—Gr. 3
Wyndmere Elementary
Wyndmere, ND

Binding Class Books

Bind class books in a jiffy with the help of plastic cable ties (available at hardware stores). Simply hole-punch the project and then thread a cable tie through each opening and lock it—leaving plenty of room for the pages of the book to be turned. Snip off any excess plastic at the end of each tie and the class book is ready to read!

Suzanne Gerczynski—Gr. 1
Glen Burnie Park Elementary
Glen Burnie, MD

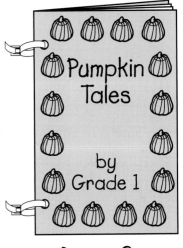

Nifty Napkin Covers

Serve up **writing inspiration** on paper napkins. Give each child a seasonal or theme-related napkin and several sheets of paper cut to fit inside the folded napkin. Provide a writing prompt or two. A student writes and illustrates her story. Then she staples her work inside her folded napkin. Now that's fine writing!

Linda Macke—Gr. 2
John F. Kennedy Elementary
Kettering, OH

Time for a Picnic!

Friendly Letter Puzzle

Piece together a perfect review of the **friendly letter format!** On a piece of poster board, write a friendly letter. Laminate the letter for durability and then cut it into five puzzle pieces that each show a different part of the letter. Use a permanent marker to label the back of each piece for self-checking. Store the pieces in an envelope and place the envelope at a center. A student assembles the letter, reads each letter part, names it, and then flips the puzzle piece to confirm his answer.

Kristy Osborn—Gr. 3
Abraham Lincoln School, Indianapolis, IN

An Important Farewell

Let Margaret Wise Brown's *The Important Book* create the framework for a **farewell writing** activity. During an oral reading, emphasize the pattern that is established in the book. Next, ask each child to use the identified pattern to write about the important traits of a classmate (or student teacher) who is leaving. Bind the students' work into a class book that can be given as a heartwarming parting gift.

Diane Rinehard—Gr. 2
Beechgrove Elementary
Independence, KY

Famous Folks

Try a shapely and systematic approach to **famous people reports!** Give each child a five-page writing booklet in the shape of a famous person's profile. Starting with the first page and continuing in order, instruct students to label the top of each booklet page with the five Ws: Who? What? When? Where? and Why? Also display a poster like the one shown that provides a more complete writing prompt for each booklet page. To complete his report, a student responds to each prompt by writing one or more complete sentences on the corresponding page in his booklet. The shapely writing booklets increase the appeal of the project, and the systematic approach to writing the report guarantees student success.

Colleen Proffitt—Gr. 2, Doe Elementary
Mountain City, TN

Famous Person Report
Answer these questions in your report.
• Who is the person?
• What did the person do to become famous?
• When did each event take place?
• Where did each event take place?
• Why did the person choose to do these things?

Martin Luther King Jr.

Dream Pets

What pets do your youngsters dream of having? Find out during National Pet Week, the first full week in May. Have each child illustrate, name, and describe her dream pet on provided paper. Then post the **paragraph projects** with the title "Dreaming About Pets."

Yvonne Lamb
Oshawa, Ontario, Canada

Writing Portfolios

Use a color-coded system for **portfolios** that clearly shows parents how a piece of writing progresses from start to finish. For example, have students use green paper for brainstorming or planning, yellow paper for first drafts, and white paper for final drafts. Now that's a bright idea!

Colleen Dabney
Williamsburg-JCC Public Schools
Williamsburg, VA

Stick 'em Up!

If you're tired of distributing and collecting your students' **journals** every day, try this! Purchase a mini suction cup with a hook for each of your students. Attach each suction cup to a window or other smooth surface, such as a file cabinet or a bookcase. Using a hole puncher, punch a hole in the top of each child's journal; then assign each child a hook on which to hang his journal. Students are responsible for their own journals, and the need for storage space is eliminated.

Grace A. Plyser, Miami, FL

A Large Letter

Help your youngsters keep their **letter-writing skills** in top form with a giant class-written letter. Ask students to dictate a class letter. Then copy the letter—in correct form—on a brightly colored length of bulletin board paper. Mount the letter so that it can be seen from each child's desk. Write the different parts of a letter on individual sentence strips; then attach the strips to the appropriate locations on the class-dictated letter. Encourage students to refer to the giant letter as they pen letters to their pals.

Beth Martin Sine—Gr. 3
Dr. Brown Elementary
Waldorf, MD

Author, Author!

Personalize your students' literary works with **pictures of the authors.** Photocopy a supply of your students' school pictures. Each time a child publishes a book, have the child glue one of her pictures to the inside cover. For an added touch, have the child write a few sentences about herself below the picture.

Olga Mendoza—Gr. 1
Cedar Grove Elementary
El Paso, TX

Clear Pocket Book Display

This clever **bookbinding** idea allows you to assemble class books and then take them apart without damaging individual pages. To make a book, bind together several clear 10" x 12" plastic sleeves. (Plastic comb binding is desirable.) Slip a decorated construction paper cover into the first and last sleeves; then slip a child's story page into each remaining sleeve. Because the plastic sleeves protect your students' stories, the stories will be in perfect condition when it's time to take them home.

Cam Gerdts—Grs. 1–2
Minnesota Lake Elementary
Minnesota Lake, MN

A Second Printing

Your young authors will be as pleased as punch with this **publishing** suggestion. Explain that for this year's final community service project you would like each child to republish a favorite story he has written. Tell students that the stories will be given to the children's ward at a local hospital. Provide the needed supplies and make arrangements for the books to be delivered. Your authors will be bursting with pride!

Cathy Rike—Gr. 1
Jefferson Elementary
Winston-Salem, NC

A Journal a Day

Wrap up the year with this **journal-a-day writing program!** Ask each child to donate a 9" x 12" spiral notebook. Label the first page of each notebook with a different writing topic; then tape a class list to each front cover. A student receives a different journal each day. He crosses his name from the class list and then writes in the journal on the provided topic. For added writing motivation, read two or three journal entries aloud each day. When the writing project is complete, display the journals in the classroom library for further reading enjoyment.

Becky Shelley—Gr. 1
Anderson Elementary, Anderson, MO

Writing Topic
Write about a time that you felt very, very proud.

Sustained Silent Writing

Promote writing by using a variation of the familiar sustained silent reading technique designed to encourage reading. Set aside a 15- to 20-minute period of time each day for writing. Students may write about the events of the day, an assigned writing topic, or topics of their own choosing. Model the importance of writing during this activity by engaging in writing yourself. Because all energies are focused on writing, creativity is sure to flourish!

Nancy Murray—Gr. 2
Forest Hills Primary, Walterboro, SC

Year-End Magazine

If you're interested in publishing a student-authored class magazine as a **year-end writing project,** here's the scoop! Begin with a list of student-suggested departments, such as "On the Road," "School News," "Scientific Discoveries," "Fashion Runway," "Most Read Books," and "Funniest Moments." Assign a committee of writers to work on each magazine department. When a committee is in agreement about what to include in its department, the committee submits a plan to you, the editor, for approval. When approval is granted, the writing begins. After a final copy of each magazine department is received from each committee, organize the writing and publish it in magazine form for each child. Students are sure to treasure these impressive keepsakes of their school year.

Kathleen McShea—Gr. 3
Public School 76
Long Island City, NY

Remember When...

This **end-of-the-year project** results in a class book of memories that students and parents will treasure for years to come. Invite students to share their fondest memories from the past year. List their responses on the board, starting each one with "Remember when." When you have several ideas listed, have each child copy one memory from the list on provided paper, write a few sentences about it, and render a black-and-white illustration of it. Make a class supply of each student's completed page. Then collate and bind the pages so that each child has a book of his own. Invite your youngsters to take the books home and color them. No doubt this class book will receive rave reviews!

Ruth Heller—Gr. 3
P.S. 156, Laurelton, NY

Remember when we made a class cookbook? We each brought a recipe from home. Then we copied the recipe and drew a picture of what it made. My mom loves this cookbook!

Summer Letter Writing

Inspire students to maintain their writing skills during summer break by giving each child a small gift and a promise. To prepare each gift, place three decorated sheets of stationery and a stamped, self-addressed envelope in a decorated bag. Distribute the bags on the last day of school. Invite each child to **write a friendly letter** to you this summer. Suggest that students describe special summer happenings in their letters. Promise to reply to each letter that you receive. It may be as much of a treat for you to read about your students' summer adventures as it will be for them to get letters from you!

Debbie Tofflemire—Gr. 1
West Indianola School
Topeka, KS

Mrs. Debbie Tofflemire
123 Main Street
Topeka, KS 12345

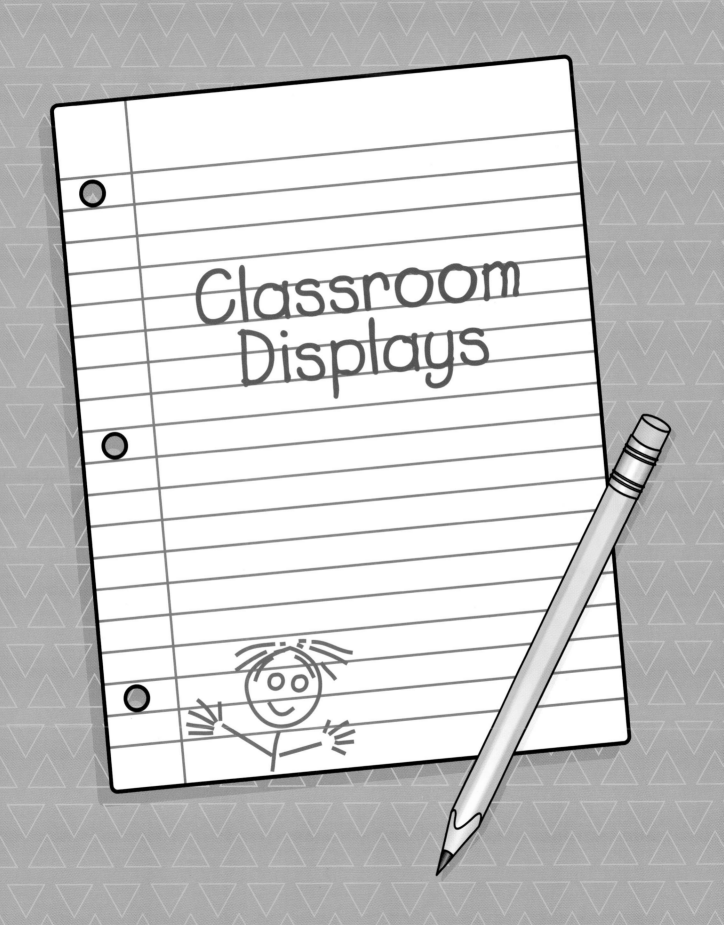

CLASSROOM DISPLAYS

It's full steam ahead for reinforcing writing skills year-round! When a child produces writing that is on track, invite him to copy his work on a form like the one shown. Mount the writing sample on a boxcar fashioned from a 9" x 12" sheet of colorful construction paper. "Choo-choo-choose" to continually update this trainload of precious cargo!

Esther Heilpern—Gr. 2, Bais Esther School, Brooklyn, NY

This travel display is quite a sight! Ask each student to ponder the places she visited over the summer as she personalizes, colors, and cuts out a car-shaped paper topper (see pattern on page 112). Then have her write and illustrate a story about one place she visited. Display the students' stories and paper toppers as shown. Invite students to continue their travels by reading about their classmates' trips!

adapted from an idea by Angie Kelley—Gr. 3, Weaver Elementary School, Anniston, AL

You can count on this easy-to-create display being a huge hit with your students. To create a booklet holder for each child, staple the sides and lower edge of a one-foot strip of green, corrugated bulletin board border to the display. Each student slips a completed booklet containing a dinosaur story into a holder. The "dino-mite" tales are now "dino-mite" reading selections!

Kathy Quinlan—Gr. 2, Charles E. Bennett Elementary, Green Cove Springs, FL

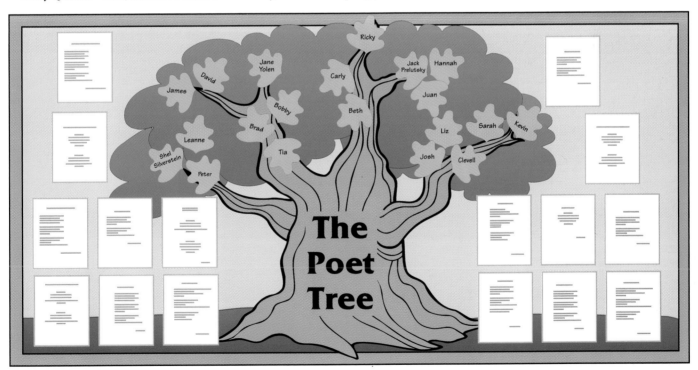

Invite budding poets to go out on a limb and publish their prose under "The Poet Tree." Mount a tree-shaped cutout, the title, and a few paper leaves labeled with the names of poets your students will recognize. When a student is ready to showcase an original poem at the display, attach a leaf bearing her name to the tree. Encourage students to periodically replace their poems with more current samples.

Karen Dubé Lamas—Grs. 1–5 Gifted, Campbell Drive Elementary, Miami, FL

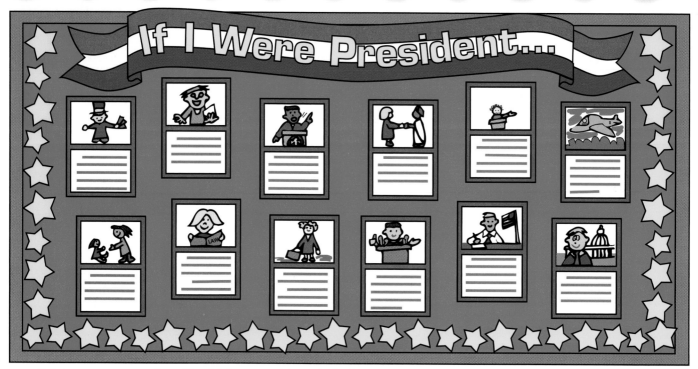

Salute your youngsters' presidential dreams at this patriotic display. On an 8" x 10" sheet of white paper, have each child illustrate herself as president of the United States. Then, on a sheet of 8" x 10" writing paper, have each youngster write a story that begins "If I were president…" Mount each student's completed projects on a large sheet of colorful construction paper and display the student work as shown. Now that's impressive!

Linda Hilliard—Grs. 1–3, Arlington, VA

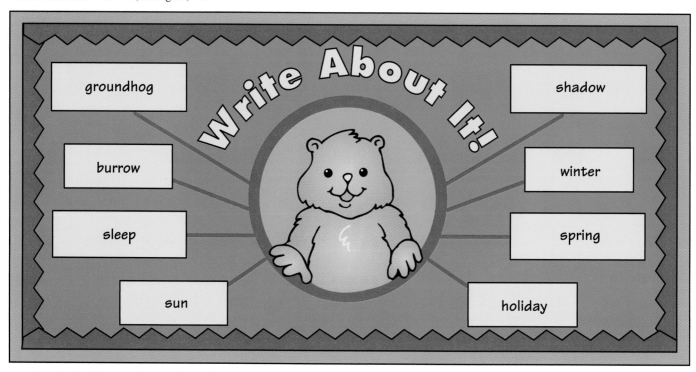

Provide budding authors with oodles of writing inspiration! Laminate blank cards and a circle and then display them as shown. Mount a visual writing prompt in the circle. Use a wipe-off marker to label the cards with student-provided words that relate to the prompt. You'll have writers eager to write and a web that's easy to adapt!

Robin Hartnett—Gr. 3, Grosse Pointe Academy, Grosse Pointe Farms, MI

Students warm right up to this patchwork project! Cover a bulletin board with assorted fabric swatches and add a title. (If desired, invite students to supply precut swatches that represent their families.) Then have each child pen a paragraph about a favorite family tradition. Mount each student's work on construction paper before adding it to the display. The resulting quilt is definitely a classy keepsake!

Cami Shapiro—Gr. 2, Taylor Mills School, Manalapan, NJ

Reinforce the teachings of Martin Luther King Jr. with this patriotic display! Review Dr. King's dream for peace, understanding, and freedom. Then ask each child to write and illustrate a sentence that describes one way she upholds his teachings. Showcase the youngsters' work for others to admire.

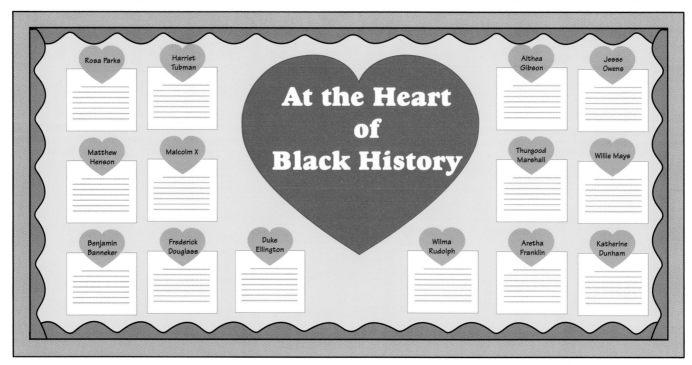

Get to the heart of Black History Month! Give each student a small paper heart labeled with the name of a famous Black American. Instruct her to learn about the person's contributions to black history and then describe them on provided paper. Showcase the student projects as shown. Impressive!

Sharma Houston—Gr. 2, Pearsontown Elementary, Durham, NC

A wee bit of writing motivation quickly creates this eye-catching display! Mount a writing prompt and leprechaun character as shown. Ask each child to write and illustrate a story in response to the prompt. Then exhibit each child's work with a personalized shamrock cutout. And here's a bit of luck for you! Simply update the writing prompt and artwork each month and you have a year-round display.

Tiffany Gosseen—Gr. 1, North Nodaway R-VI Elementary, Hopkins, MO

Bring the community into focus at this informative display! Each child writes a brief report about a community landmark and mounts it on construction paper. Then she folds her project in half (keeping the writing inside), tapes a snapshot of the location on the front, and glues a camera cutout (pattern on page 112) over the photo so that the landmark is seen through the lens opening. Mount the picture-perfect projects as shown.

Kathleen Cowin—Gr. 2, Munson Primary School, Mulvane, KS

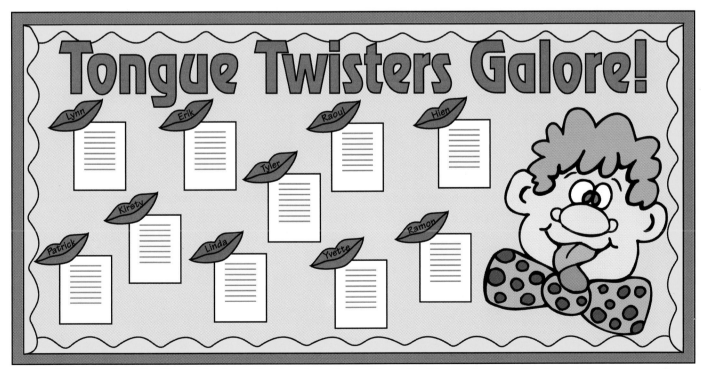

You'll create miles of writing motivation with this unique display. Mount the title and character; then have each youngster write a collection of tongue twisters. After the twisters have been edited and recopied, attach them to the display. For added fun, staple a pair of personalized lip cutouts to each child's paper. Invite students to update their tongue twister collections as often as desired.

Kristin Goss—Gr. 3, Weigelstown Elementary, Manchester, PA

Candy
Sweet, smooth, crunchy.
My mouth waters for it.
I love chocolate most of all.
Yummy!
Sam Smith

April, National Poetry Month, is a perfect time to sweeten students' poetry-writing skills! To make the display, attach a paper cutout resembling the end of wrapped candy to each side of a paper-covered board. Have each child write and publish a candy-related cinquain (or another form of poetry) and showcase the poems as shown. Attach a colorful candy sticker to each one if desired. Now that's a delicious twist!

Tracy Welsch—Gr. 2, Camp Avenue Elementary School, North Merrick, NY

Spotlight your youngsters' weekend experiences at this eye-catching display. Each Monday, every child who has a weekend experience that she'd like to share with the class creates an illustration and a caption about it. Showcase these projects and set aside time for each child to explain her work and provide added details about the pictured event.

Donna L. Hall—Grs. 1–2, Fairview Elementary, St. Louis, MO